Maths Progress Tests for White Rose

Year 6/P7

Rachel Axten-Higgs

William Collins' dream of knowledge for all began with the publication of his first book in 1819. A self-educated mill worker, he not only enriched millions of lives, but also founded a flourishing publishing house. Today, staying true to this spirit, Collins books are packed with inspiration, innovation and practical expertise. They place you at the centre of a world of possibility and give you exactly what you need to explore it.

Collins. Freedom to teach.

Collins
An imprint of HarperCollins*Publishers*
The News Building
1 London Bridge Street
London
SE1 9GF

MIX
Paper from responsible sources
FSC
www.fsc.org
FSC™ C007454

This book is produced from independently certified FSC™ paper to ensure responsible forest management.

For more information visit: **www.harpercollins.co.uk/green**

Browse the complete Collins catalogue at
www.collins.co.uk

10 9 8 7 6 5 4 3 2 1

ISBN 978-0-00-833358-4

British Library Cataloguing in Publication Data. A catalogue record for this publication is available from the British Library.

Author: Rachel Axten-Higgs
Publisher: Katie Sergeant
Commissioning Editor: Fiona Lazenby
Product Developer: Mike Appleton
Copyeditor: Joan Miller
Proofreader: Catherine Dakin
Design and Typesetting: Ken Vail Graphic Design
Cover Design: The Big Mountain Design
Production controller: Katharine Willard
Printed and bound by CPI Group (UK) Ltd, Croydon, CR0 4YY

Contents

How to use this book

Introduction

Collins Maths Progress Tests for White Rose have been designed to give you a consistent whole-school approach to teaching and assessing mathematics. Each photocopiable book covers the required mathematics objectives from the 2014 Primary English National Curriculum. For teachers in Scotland, the books can offer guidance and structure that is not provided in the Curriculum for Excellence Experiences and Outcomes or Benchmarks for Numeracy and Mathematics.

As stand-alone tests, the *Collins Maths Progress Tests for White Rose* provide a structured way to assess progress in arithmetic and reasoning skills, to help you identify areas for development, and to provide evidence towards expectations for each year group. Whilst the tests are independent of any textbook-based teaching and learning scheme to allow for maximum flexibility, the content for each test has been selected based on the suggested teaching order in the *White Rose Maths Schemes of Learning*, which are designed to support a mastery approach to teaching and learning.

Assessment of mathematical skills

At the end of KS1 and KS2, children sit tests to assess the standards they have reached in mathematics. This is done through national curriculum tests (SATs) in Arithmetic and Mathematical Reasoning. *Collins Maths Progress Tests for White Rose* have been designed to provide children with opportunities to explore a range of question types whilst building familiarity with the format, language and style of the SATs.

The Arithmetic tests comprise constructed response questions, presented as context-free calculations, to assess pupils' confidence with a range of mathematics operations as appropriate to the year group. Questions come from the Number, Ratio and Algebra domains.

The Reasoning tests present mathematical problems in a wide range of formats to ensure pupils can fully demonstrate mathematical fluency, mathematical problem solving and mathematical reasoning. They include both selected response questions (e.g. multiple choice, matching, yes/no) and constructed response questions. Questions may draw on all content domains and approximately half of the questions in the Reasoning tests are presented in context.

The tests follow the structure and format of SATs mathematics papers and are pitched at a level appropriate to age-related expectations for the year group. They provide increasing challenge within each year group and across the school, both in terms of content and cognitive demand, but also with increasing numbers of questions to build stamina and resilience. Using the progress tests with your classes at the end of each half-term should help pupils to develop and practise the necessary skills required to complete the national tests with confidence, as well as offering you a snapshot of their progress at those points throughout the year. You can use the results formatively to help identify gaps in knowledge and next teaching steps.

How to use this book

In this book, you will find twelve photocopiable tests: one arithmetic test and one reasoning test for use at the end of each half term of teaching. Each child will need a copy of the test. You will find Curriculum Content Coverage on page vi indicating the White Rose Scheme of Learning Block and associated Content Domain topics covered in each test across the year group. The specific Content Domain references indicating the year, strand and substrand, e.g. 2N1, for the questions in each test are in the tables on page 107. You may find it useful to make a photocopy of these tables for each child and highlight questions answered incorrectly to help identify any consistent areas of difficulty.

The number of marks available and suggested timing to be allowed are indicated for each test. The number of marks/questions in each test and the length of time allowed increases gradually across the year as summarised in the table below. Note that the Year 2 and Year 6 Summer term tests have been written as full practice papers assuming that all content will have been taught by this point. They mirror the number of marks and time allowed in the end of Key Stage 1 and end of Key Stage 2 test papers.

Year group	Test	Time allowed	Number of marks
6	Autumn 1 Arithmetic	27 minutes	35
6	Autumn 1 Reasoning	35 minutes	30
6	Autumn 2 Arithmetic	30 minutes	35
6	Autumn 2 Reasoning	35 minutes	30
6	Spring 1 Arithmetic	30 minutes	40
6	Spring 1 Reasoning	35 minutes	35
6	Spring 2 Arithmetic	30 minutes	40
6	Spring 2 Reasoning	35 minutes	35
6	Summer 1 Arithmetic	30 minutes	40
6	Summer 1 Reasoning	40 minutes	35
6	Summer 2 Arithmetic	30 minutes	40
6	Summer 2 Reasoning	40 minutes	35

To help you mark the tests, you will find mark schemes at the back of the book. These include the answer requirement, number of marks to be awarded, additional guidance on answers that should or should not be accepted and when to award marks for working in multi-mark questions.

Test demand

The tests have been written to assess progress in children's arithmetic and mathematical reasoning skills with the content and cognitive demand of questions increasing within each book and across the series to build towards to end of key stage expectations of the SATs. Since the national tests may cover content from the whole key stage, each progress test contains some questions which draw on content from earlier terms or previous year objectives (particularly in autumn term tests). This ensures that prior content and skills are revisited.

The level of demand for each question has been provided within the mark schemes for each test using the notation T (working towards), E (expected standard) or G (greater depth). These ratings are given as an indication of the level of complexity of each question taking into account the thinking skills required to understand what is being asked, the computational complexity in calculating the answer, spatial reasoning or data interpretation required and the response strategy for the question.

Performance thresholds

The table below provides guidance for assessing how children perform in the tests. Most children should achieve scores at or above the expected standard, with some children working at greater depth and exceeding expectations for their year group. While the thresholds bands do not represent standardised scores, as in the end of key stage SATs, they will give an indication of how pupils are performing against the expected standards for their year group. The thresholds have been set broadly assuming that pupils who achieve greater than 60% will be working at the expected standard and those who

score more than 80% are likely to be working at greater depth. However, pupils will all have individual strengths and weaknesses, so it is possible that they could be working towards the expected standard in some areas but at greater depth in others. For this reason, using the content domain coverage tables to identify common areas of difficulty alongside your own professional judgement, will enable you to identify pupils' specific gaps in knowledge and areas where further teaching may be required.

Tracking progress

A record sheet is provided to help you illustrate to children the areas in which their arithmetic and reasoning skills are strong and where they need to develop. A spreadsheet tracker is also provided via collins.co.uk/assessment/downloads which enables you to identify whole-class patterns of attainment. This can be used to inform your next teaching and learning steps.

Editable download

All the files are available online in Word and PDF format. Go to collins.co.uk/assessment/downloads to find instructions on how to download. The files are password protected and the password clue is included on the website. You will need to use the clue to locate the password in your book.

You can use these editable files to help you meet the specific needs of your class, whether that be by increasing or decreasing the challenge, by reducing the number of questions, by providing more space for answers or increasing the size of text for specific children.

Year group	Test	Working towards (T)	Expected standard (E)	Greater depth (G)
6	Autumn 1 Arithmetic	20 marks or below	21–27 marks	28–35 marks
6	Autumn 1 Reasoning	17 marks or below	18–23 marks	24–30 marks
6	Autumn 2 Arithmetic	20 marks or below	21–27 marks	28–35 marks
6	Autumn 2 Reasoning	17 marks or below	18–23 marks	24–30 marks
6	Spring 1 Arithmetic	23 marks or below	24–31 marks	32–40 marks
6	Spring 1 Reasoning	20 marks or below	21–27 marks	28–35 marks
6	Spring 2 Arithmetic	23 marks or below	24–31 marks	32–40 marks
6	Spring 2 Reasoning	20 marks or below	21–27 marks	28–35 marks
6	Summer 1 Arithmetic	23 marks or below	24–31 marks	32–40 marks
6	Summer 1 Reasoning	20 marks or below	21–27 marks	28–35 marks
6	Summer 2 Arithmetic	23 marks or below	24–31 marks	32–40 marks
6	Summer 2 Reasoning	20 marks or below	21–27 marks	28–35 marks

Curriculum content coverage

All content objectives from the Year 6 National Curriculum Programme of Study for Mathematics are covered within one or more of the half-termly progress tests across the year. The content for each test is based on the suggested teaching order of the White Rose Maths Schemes of Learning. The table below shows from which teaching blocks the content for each test is drawn. Where the White Rose Maths blocks are devoted to skills or consolidation rather than introduction of new content, these blocks are not covered by the tests. The Summer tests for Year 6 draw on content from previous blocks to offer full SATs practice tests.

White Rose Schemes of Learning blocks			Autumn 1: Arithmetic	Autumn 1: Reasoning	Autumn 2: Arithmetic	Autumn 2: Reasoning	Spring 1: Arithmetic	Spring 1: Reasoning	Spring 2: Arithmetic	Spring 2: Reasoning	Summer 1: Arithmetic	Summer 1: Reasoning	Summer 2: Arithmetic	Summer 2: Reasoning
Blocks	**Weeks**	**Topics**												
Autumn Block 1	Weeks 1–2	Number: Place Value	✔	✔							✔	✔	✔	✔
Autumn Block 2	Weeks 3–6	Number: Four Operations (Addition, Subtraction, Multiplication, Division)	✔	✔	✔	✔					✔	✔	✔	✔
Autumn Block 3	Weeks 7–10	Number: Fractions			✔	✔					✔	✔	✔	✔
Autumn Block 4	Week 11	Geometry: Position and direction				✔						✔		✔
Autumn Block 5	Week 12	Consolidation												
Spring Block 1	Weeks 1–2	Number: Decimals					✔	✔	✔		✔	✔	✔	✔
Spring Block 2	Weeks 3–4	Number: Percentages					✔	✔	✔		✔	✔	✔	✔
Spring Block 3	Weeks 5–6	Number: Algebra					✔	✔	✔		✔	✔	✔	✔
Spring Block 4	Week 7	Measurement: Converting Units								✔		✔		✔
Spring Block 5	Weeks 8–9	Measurement: Perimeter, Area and Volume								✔		✔		✔
Spring Block 6	Weeks 10–11	Number: Ratio							✔	✔	✔	✔	✔	✔
Spring Block 7	Week 12	Consolidation												
Summer Block 1	Weeks 1–2	Geometry: Properties of Shape										✔		✔
Summer Block 2	Weeks 3–5	Problem Solving												
Summer Block 3	Weeks 6–7	Statistics										✔		✔
Summer Block 4	Weeks 8–11	Investigations												
Summer Block 5	Week 12	Consolidation												

Collins Maths Progress Tests for White Rose

Name _____

1 $4,567 \div 1 =$

1 mark

2 $180 \div 5 =$

1 mark

3 $746 - \boxed{} = 737$

1 mark

4 $\dfrac{3}{8} + \dfrac{4}{8} =$

1 mark

5 $5,700 + \boxed{} = 6,600$

1 mark

6 $743 \times 7 =$

1 mark

7 $\boxed{} + 100 = 476$

1 mark

8 $17.6 - 9.46 =$

1 mark

9 $4^3 =$

1 mark

10 $225 \div 25 =$

1 mark

11 $70 - (7 \times 7) =$

1 mark

12 $450 \div 30 =$

1 mark

Name _____

13 $4,890 \times 1,000 =$

1 mark

14

| 4 | 0 | 1 | 5 | 8 | 9 |

1 mark

15 $72 \div 9 =$

1 mark

16 $504 \div 9 =$

1 mark

17 $\frac{2}{6} - \frac{1}{12} =$

1 mark

18 $4,787 + 9,212 =$

1 mark

Name _____

19 $587 \times 8 =$

1 mark

20 $35 - 5 \times 6 =$

1 mark

21 $4{,}900 \div 7 =$

1 mark

22 $70 \times 700 =$

1 mark

23

$$9\ 5\ |\ 5\ 8\ 4\ 3$$

Show your method

2 marks

24 $83 + 8 \times 9 =$

1 mark

25 $4^2 + 10 =$

1 mark

26

3 0 | 2 3 4 9

1 mark

27

$$\begin{array}{r} 9\ 4\ 5 \\ \times \qquad 3\ 2 \\ \hline \end{array}$$

Show your method   2 marks

28 $7^3 + 100 =$

1 mark

29

$$\begin{array}{r} 1\ 7\ 8\ 9 \\ \times \qquad 2\ 2 \\ \hline \end{array}$$

1 mark

30

1 7 | 7 1 4

Show your method   2 marks

31   4,070,080 = [   ] + 70,000 + 80

1 mark

32   6,000,000 + [   ] + 7 = 6,004,007

1 mark

Total marks ………../35

1 Write the missing number.

One is done for you.

345   is 100 more than   245

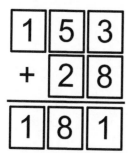   is 100 more than   687

1 mark

2 Martha completes this calculation.

```
  1 5 3
+   2 8
  1 8 1
```

Write a **subtraction** calculation she could use to check her answer.

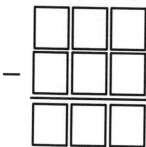

1 mark

3 Oscar has £850.

He buys a remote-controlled dinosaur for £287 and a robot for £350.

How much money does he have left?

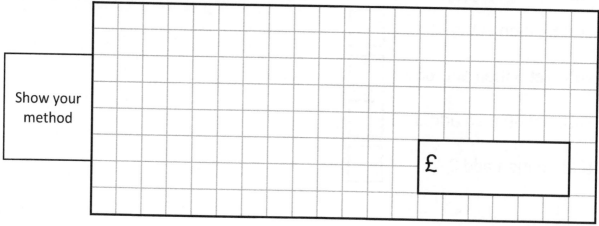

Show your method

£ _____

2 marks

4 Write the missing numbers to make this **multiplication** grid correct.

×		
9	81	54
7	63	

5 Tick all the prime numbers in the list below.

2 ☐   12 ☐

3 ☐   13 ☐

4 ☐   17 ☐

5 ☐   18 ☐

7 ☐   19 ☐

8 ☐

6 Freddie wants to use a mental method to calculate 195 + 63.

He starts from 195.

Here are some methods Freddie could use.

Tick **all** the methods that are **correct**.

add 65 then subtract 2   ☐

subtract 5 then add 65   ☐

subtract 60 then add 3   ☐

add 60 then add 3   ☐

7

| A | £24,897 | B | £89,876 | C | £16,054 | D | £109,786 | E | £99,789 |

Put these cars in order of price, starting with the **highest price**.
One has been done for you.

_____   _____   _____   __A__   _____

highest

1 mark

8 The numbers in this sequence **increase** by the same amount each time.

678,680   678,780   678,880   678,980   _____

What is the next number in the sequence?

[   ]

1 mark

9 Imran does an experiment by measuring the temperature outside in two separate seasons.

In January the reading he takes is –4 °C.

In July the reading he takes is 23 °C.

Find the difference in temperature. Draw a number line to show your method.

_____

[°C   ]

2 marks

9

10 At a museum, the year it was built is written above the door.

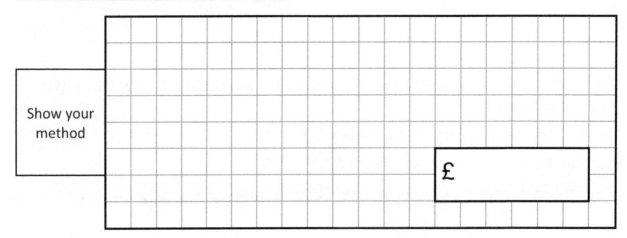

MCMXC

Write the year MCMXC in **figures**.

[   ]

1 mark

11 Large cuddly toys cost £14.99.

Medium cuddly toys cost £9.59.

Small cuddly toys cost £4.99.

Freya buys 1 large, 1 medium and 2 small cuddly toys.

She has saved £36 pocket money.

How much change does she get?

Show your method

£

2 marks

12 Round 2,156,789

to the nearest 100   [   ]

to the nearest 10,000   [   ]

to the nearest 1,000,000   [   ]

2 marks

13

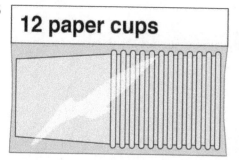 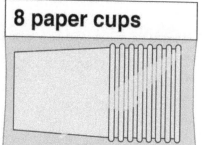

Sam buys 6 packs of 8 paper cups.

Mika buys 3 packs of 12 paper cups.

Sam says: 'I have twice as many cups as Mika.'

Explain why Sam is not correct.

1 mark

14 Write three factors of 30 that are not factors of 50.

2 marks

15 Suni has put five 6-digit numbers in order.

The smallest number is 126,780.

The largest number is 136,020.

Each of the other numbers has a digit total of 20 and no repeating digits.

What could the other three numbers be?

2 marks

16 5,304 ÷ 13 = 408

Explain how you can use this fact to find the answer to **14 × 408**.

1 mark

17 This is a list of ingredients for a cake.

flour   250 g
sugar   250 g
eggs   5
butter 200 g
cocoa   30 g

Luigi has only 200 g of flour to make the cake.

How much **cocoa** should he use?

Show your method

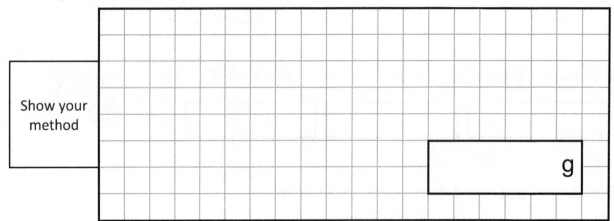

Show your
method

g

2 marks

18 | < | = | > |

Write the correct symbol in each box to make the statements correct.

| 12 × 7 | ☐ | 13 × 6 |

| 75 ÷ 25 | ☐ | 80 ÷ 20 |

| 270 ÷ 9 | ☐ | 320 ÷ 8 |

| 40 × 5 | ☐ | 10 × 17 |

2 marks

19 The base of Buckingham Palace has an area of 12,960 square metres.

The base of the White House is 26 metres long by 51 metres wide.

How much larger is the base area of Buckingham Palace than the base area of the White House?

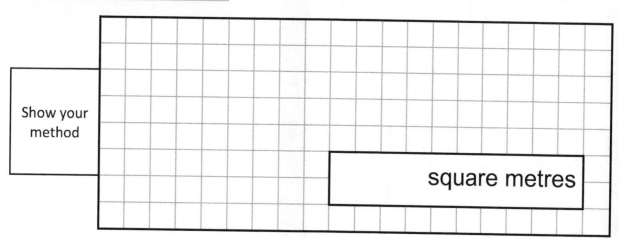

Show your method

square metres

3 marks

Total marks ..../30

1　170 + 1,000 =

1 mark

2　22 − 7.9 =

1 mark

3　59,896 − 5,679 =

1 mark

4　1,784 ÷ 6 =

1 mark

5　63.9 − 17.354 =

1 mark

6　512 × 100 =

1 mark

　　　　　14

7	$67.9 - 12.805 =$

1 mark

8	$\frac{48}{100} - \frac{29}{100} =$

1 mark

9	$8,000,000 - 7 =$

1 mark

10	$2,536,109 + 60,000 =$

1 mark

11	$70 + (64 \div 8) =$

1 mark

12	$\frac{3}{5} \times 110$

1 mark

13 5,879,520 + 600,000 =

1 mark

14 749 × 9 =

1 mark

15 $\frac{1}{4}$ × 100 =

1 mark

16 $\frac{1}{4}$ × $\frac{4}{5}$ =

1 mark

17 $\frac{1}{4}$ ÷ 2 =

1 mark

18 $8^3 - 24$ =

1 mark

19 $17.8 - 9.456$

1 mark

20 $116 - 72 \div 9 =$

1 mark

21 $5\frac{4}{5} - 2\frac{4}{12} =$

1 mark

22 $4^2 + 10 =$

1 mark

23 $\frac{7}{10} - \frac{2}{20} =$

1 mark

24 $90 - 8 \times 9 =$

1 mark

25 $\frac{6}{8} \div 3 =$

1 mark

26 $\frac{3}{4} \div 4 =$

1 mark

27 $\frac{1}{4} + \frac{3}{8} + \frac{7}{12} =$

1 mark

28 $3\frac{1}{4} + \frac{9}{10} =$

1 mark

29

1 3 | 5 8 5

Show your method   2 marks

30

```
    3 9 6 7
×         3 2
```

Show your method   2 marks

31

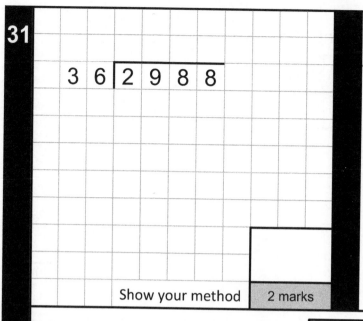

$$3 \: 6 \: | \: 2 \: 9 \: 8 \: 8$$

Show your method | 2 marks

32

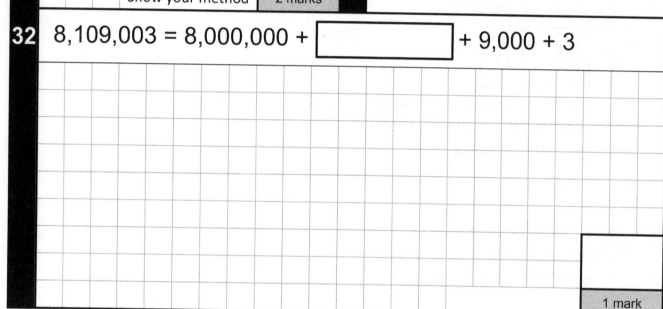

$$8{,}109{,}003 = 8{,}000{,}000 + \boxed{} + 9{,}000 + 3$$

1 mark

Total marks ..../35

19

1 These diagrams show three equivalent fractions.

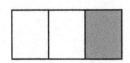 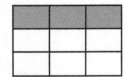

Write the missing values.

$$\frac{1}{3} = \frac{3}{\square} = \frac{\square}{18}$$

1 mark

2 Sabina uses **3** digit cards.

She makes a two-digit number and a one-digit number.
She multiples the numbers together.
Her answer is a **multiple of 10**.

What could Sabina's multiplication be?

1 mark

3 A box contains trays of eggs.
There are 24 eggs in a tray.
There are 6 trays in a box.

A shop sells **25** boxes of eggs.

How many eggs does the shop sell?

Show your
method

eggs

2 marks

4   Here are **four** number cards.

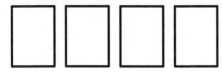

Coby uses each card once to make a four-digit number.
He places:

- 3 in the tens columns

- 9 so that it has a lower place value than any of the other digits

- The remaining two digits so that 5 has the higher place value.

Write a digit in each box to show Coby's number.

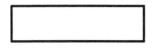

1 mark

5   Two decimal numbers add together to equal 1.

One of the numbers is 0.028

What is the other number?

1 mark

6   A model is made from 25 building bricks. 15 of the bricks are yellow and 10 of the bricks are red.

What **percentage** of the bricks in the model are red?

1 mark

7 Bottles of milk cost £1.10 each.
Packets of biscuits cost £1.05 each.
A school uses 7 bottles of milk and 6 packets of biscuits every week.
There are 28 members of staff.
They share the cost equally.

How much does each staff member pay per week, to the nearest whole penny?

_____

2 marks

8 In this rectangle, $\frac{2}{6}$ and $\frac{1}{16}$ are shaded.

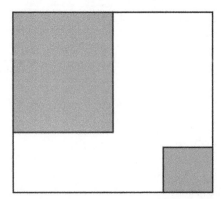

What fraction of the whole rectangle is **not** shaded?

Show your method

2 marks

9 Write the two missing values to make these equivalent fractions correct.

$$\frac{3}{9} = \frac{\boxed{}}{18} = \frac{2}{\boxed{}}$$

2 marks

10 Lucian wants to estimate the answer to this calculation.

$$5\frac{3}{5} - 3\frac{3}{4} + 2\frac{1}{6}$$

Tick the calculation below that is the best estimate.

Tick one

5 – 4 + 2   ☐

6 – 4 + 2   ☐

6 – 4 + 3   ☐

6 – 3 + 3   ☐

1 mark

11 Write all the common multiples of 3 and 5 that are **less than 50**.

_____

1 mark

12 In each box, circle the number that is **greater**.

$3\frac{3}{4}$	3.6

$3\frac{1}{3}$	3.25

$3\frac{19}{100}$	3.2

$3\frac{6}{7}$	3.7

2 marks

13 Here is a triangle drawn on a coordinate grid.

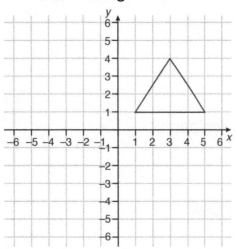

The triangle is translated **5 left** and **6 down**.

Draw the triangle in its new position.

_____
1 mark

14 35,583 = 409 × 87

Use this multiplication to complete the calculations below.

40.9 × 87 = ☐   409 × 870 = ☐   409 × 8.7 = ☐

_____
2 marks

15 Mathias is making up party bags for his son's party.
Sweets cost £1.10 per 100 g.
Toys cost 59p each.
Slime pots cost 79p each.
Party bags cost £1.50 for 12.
He makes 24 party bags, each with a slime pot, toy and 50 g of sweets inside.

Calculate the total cost to make 24 party bags.

Show your method

£

_____
3 marks

16 Write the correct symbol, <, = or >, in each box to make the statements correct.

14×19 ☐ 17×10 $250 \div 5$ ☐ $100 \div 2$

$70 \div 20$ ☐ $90 \div 30$ 100×6 ☐ 90×7

2 marks

17 The floor of a school hall measures 22 m by 18 m.
A classroom in the same school is 9 m **shorter** and 9 m **narrower** than the school hall.

What is the difference in floor area between the two rooms?

Show your method

m²

3 marks

18 Here are two **identical** shaded triangles drawn on coordinate axes.

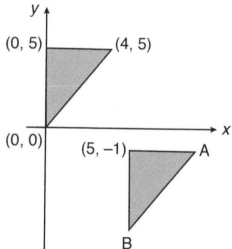

Write the coordinates of points A and B.

A = (___ , ___)   B = (___ , ___)

2 marks

Total marks ..../30

Name _____

1 $\frac{11}{12} - \frac{6}{12} =$

1 mark

2 [ ] + 100 = 678

1 mark

3 482 × 6 =

1 mark

4 8,406 − 1,000 =

1 mark

5 $\frac{5}{9} + \frac{6}{9} =$

1 mark

6 $\frac{5}{8} - \frac{1}{4} =$

1 mark

26

Name _____

7 $\frac{7}{8} \times 36 =$

1 mark

8 $120 \div 30 =$

1 mark

9 $9 - 5.834$

1 mark

10 $\frac{3}{6} + \frac{7}{9} =$

1 mark

11 $23.6 - 7.95 =$

1 mark

12 $0.065 \times 1,000 =$

1 mark

13 65% of 300 =

1 mark

14 70 + 8 × 8 =

1 mark

15 $\frac{2}{7} \div 4 =$

1 mark

16 $3\frac{4}{5} + \frac{12}{15} =$

1 mark

17 135 − 120 ÷ 8

1 mark

18 1.74 × 8 =

1 mark

19 $\frac{3}{10} \div 6 =$

1 mark

20 $0.95 \div 100$

1 mark

21 $\frac{1}{4} \times \frac{1}{2} =$

1 mark

22 6.35×7

1 mark

23 $205 + 135 \div 9 =$

1 mark

24 $2\frac{5}{9} + \frac{15}{3} =$

1 mark

25 $\dfrac{3}{7} \times \dfrac{2}{5} =$

1 mark

26 15% of 400

1 mark

27 $0.004 \times 10 =$

1 mark

28 $6\dfrac{1}{2} - 3\dfrac{6}{7} =$

1 mark

29 $7.09 \times 6 =$

1 mark

30 99% of 600 =

1 mark

Name _____

31

$$4\ 8\ \overline{)\ 2\ 9\ 0\ 4}$$

Show your method | 2 marks

32

$$\begin{array}{r} 3\ 4\ 5\ 6 \\ \times \quad\quad 9\ 8 \\ \hline \end{array}$$

Show your method | 2 marks

33

$$8\ 0\ \overline{)\ 3\ 3\ 0\ 0}$$

Show your method | 2 marks

34

$$\begin{array}{r} 9\ 7\ 5\ 3 \\ \times \quad\quad 2\ 5 \\ \hline \end{array}$$

Show your method | 2 marks

35

$$\boxed{} + 65{,}000 + 403 = 1{,}065{,}403$$

1 mark

36 $2{,}080{,}006 = 2{,}000{,}000 + \boxed{} + 6$

1 mark

Total marks ………/40

1 Samir cuts **8** metres of rope into **three** pieces.
The length of the first piece is **2.45** metres.
The length of the second piece is **2.95** metres.

Work out the length of the third piece.

Show your method

metres

2 marks

2 A rectangle is translated from position **A** to position **B**.

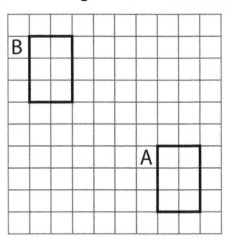

Complete the sentence.

The rectangle has moved ⬚ squares to the left and ⬚ squares up.

1 mark

3 Write each number in its correct place on the diagram.

5, 10, 11, 17, 20, 25, 32

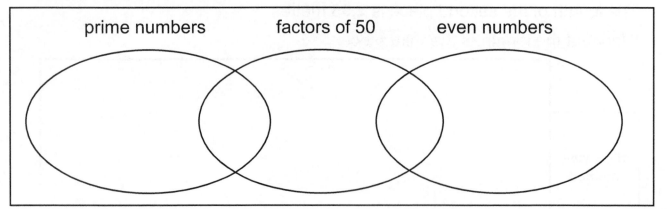

3 marks

4 Circle two numbers that add together to give a sum of 0.67

0.125   0.267   0.54   0.545

1 mark

5 Write these numbers in order, starting with the **largest.**

1.456   1.564   2.005   0.987   0.789

Largest

1 mark

6 This table shows the temperature at three different times in one morning in December.

9.30 a.m.	10.30 a.m.	11.30 a.m.
–4 °C	2.5 °C	4 °C

a) What is the difference between the temperature at 9.30 a.m. and the temperature at 11.30 a.m.?

degrees

1 mark

At 6.30 a.m. the temperature was 9 degrees lower than at 10.30 a.m..

b) What was the temperature at 6.30 a.m.?

°C

1 mark

7 Write the following number in digit form.

Sixteen million, four hundred and sixty-five thousand, eight hundred and one.

_____

8 Rufus has £550 in savings.

He spends **65%** of his money on a computer console.

How much does Rufus have left in his savings?

Show your method	
	£

9 Mr Johnson is planning a new school uniform that includes a striped tie.
The tie will have only **two** colours.
The school's colours are **red, green** and **blue.**
Write the **three** possible combinations.

_____ and _____

_____ and _____

_____ and _____

10 $\dfrac{3}{4}$ $\dfrac{2}{7}$ $\dfrac{5}{2}$

Write these fractions in order, starting with the **smallest**.

☐ ☐ ☐

Smallest

1 mark

11 Six times a number has twenty-two added to it to make 76.

a) Write the algebraic equation to work out what this number is. Use *n* as the missing number.

_____

1 mark

b) What is the missing number?

_____

1 mark

12 Isabelle is making necklaces for her friends.
Each shape of bead costs a different amount.

Cost to make = £2.22

Cost to make = £1.71

Calculate the value of each shape.

Show your working.

☆ = ☐ p   △ = ☐ p

2 marks

13 A bag contains 12 red marbles,
27 green marbles and 11 blue marbles.

a) Write the percentage of green marbles in the bag.

_____

b) Write a fraction, in its lowest form, of the number of red marbles in the bag.

_____

c) Write the decimal fraction of blue marbles in the bag.

_____

3 marks

14 278 × 65 = 18,070

Use this multiplication to complete the calculations below.

278 × 6.5 = ☐

2,780 × 65 = ☐

1,807 ÷ 65 = ☐

2 marks

15 Pam sells eggs in bags.

She uses this formula to work out how much to charge for each bag of eggs.

| Cost = number of eggs × 12p + cost of bag |

Bags cost 18p each.

How much will a bag of 9 eggs cost?

£ [ ]

Lucas buys a bag of eggs for £2.22.

Use the formula to calculate how many eggs are in the bag.

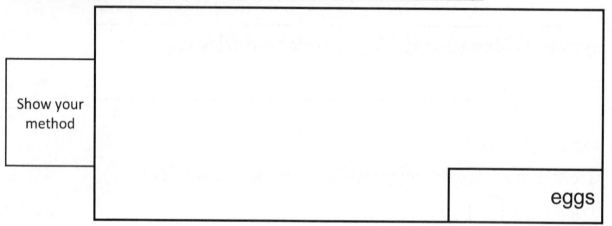

Show your method

eggs

2 marks

16 Fill in the blanks on the number line to show the decimal or fraction equivalents.

Write decimals to 3 decimal places.

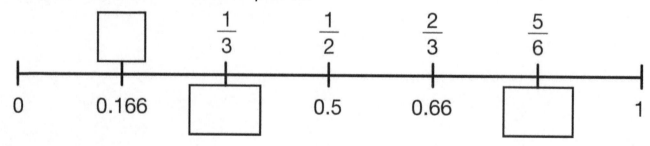

2 marks

17 Write 0.875 as a fraction.

_____
1 mark

James says that 0.8 is smaller than $\frac{9}{12}$

Explain why James is incorrect.

_____
1 mark

18 $m = 15$

What is the value of $6m - 7$?

_____
1 mark

$8s + 16 = 72$

Find the value of s.

_____
1 mark

19 Fiona is raising money for charity.`
For every £3 she raises, her uncle donates £5.
Her uncle donates a total of £45.

How much did Fiona raise before her uncle donated this money?

_____
1 mark

Total marks ………/35

1 5,608 − 10 =

1 mark

2 2,194 + 789 =

1 mark

3 3 × 6 × 9 =

1 mark

4 654 × 6

1 mark

5 5^3 =

1 mark

6 $14 \times 1\frac{2}{5}$ =

1 mark

7 $8^2 + 5 =$

1 mark

8 $17.74 + 92.9 =$

1 mark

9 $704{,}598 - 65{,}903 =$

1 mark

10 $\dfrac{7}{8} - \dfrac{7}{24} =$

1 mark

11 $\dfrac{3}{10} \times 40 =$

1 mark

12 $88 - 63 \div 7 =$

1 mark

13 35% of 1,200 =

1 mark

14 1.65 × 30 =

1 mark

15 $\frac{5}{8} \times \frac{2}{7} =$

1 mark

16 0.04 × 1,000 =

1 mark

17 18% of 200 =

1 mark

18 0.4 ÷ 100 =

1 mark

Name _____

19 $6\frac{4}{6} + 2\frac{3}{4} =$

1 mark

20 56% of 900 =

1 mark

21 $\frac{6}{8} \div 4 =$

1 mark

22 $49 + 12 \times 8 =$

1 mark

23 $\frac{5}{9} \div 5 =$

1 mark

24 $7\frac{5}{8} - 2\frac{1}{4} =$

1 mark

25 $7.03 \times 65 =$

1 mark

26 88% of 1,500

1 mark

27 $\frac{6}{13} \div 7 =$

1 mark

28 $7^2 - 56 \div 7$

1 mark

29 72% of 1,750 =

1 mark

30
$$\begin{array}{r} 2\ 0\ 6\ 0 \\ \times \qquad 7\ 7 \\ \hline \end{array}$$

Show your method   2 marks

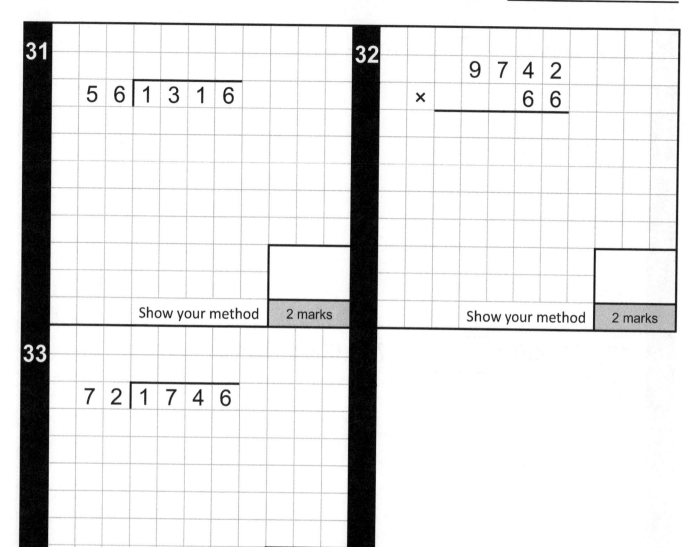

31 5 6 | 1 3 1 6

Show your method   2 marks

32
```
    9 7 4 2
  ×     6 6
```

Show your method   2 marks

33 7 2 | 1 7 4 6

Show your method   2 marks

34 6,000,000 + 40,000 + ☐ = 6,040,056

1 mark

35 $4,000,000 + \boxed{} + 106 = 4,007,106$

1 mark

36 $12,701,000 = \boxed{} + 700,000 + 1,000$

1 mark

1 Fill in the missing numbers.

84 months = ☐ years

120 hours = ☐ days

105 days = ☐ weeks

‾‾‾‾‾
2 marks

2 A clock shows this time in the afternoon.

Tick the digital clock that shows the same time.

02:45		14:45		15:15

03:15		15:45

‾‾‾‾‾
1 mark

3 Harley uses exactly 64 small cubes to make a larger cube.

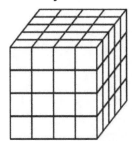

Write the letter of the **cuboid** that has the **same** volume as Harley's cube.

A   **B**   **C**   **D**   **E**

 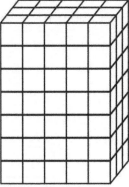 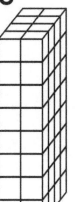 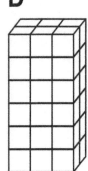 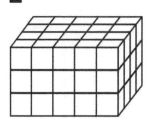

☐

‾‾‾‾‾
1 mark

4 Circle two numbers that add together to give a sum of 0.85.

0.06   0.079   0.6   0.79   0.025

5 On a map, 1 cm represents 15 km.
The distance between two towns is 120 km.

On the same map, what is the distance between the two towns?

Show your
method

cm

2 marks

6 Francesca and Rachel
buy some beads.

Francesca buys a pack of
36 beads for £2.60.
Rachel buys 8 packs of 5 beads
for 45p each.

How much more does Rachel
pay than Francesca?

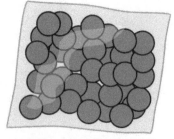

Pack of 36 beads
£2.60

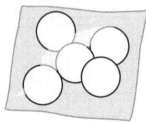

Pack of 5 beads
45p

Show your
method

£

2 marks

7 Sabini receives £1.80 pocket
money each week.
She has saved £48.60.

How many weeks has Sabini been saving?

Show your method	

8 The height of a horse (from the top of its head to its hooves) can be
estimated by:
• measuring the length of its tail
• then multiplying that length by 4.5.

What is the difference in the estimated heights of these two horses?

37 cm   40 cm

Show your method		p

9   **Seven metres** of ribbons cost £4.20.

What is the cost of **one centimetre** of ribbon?

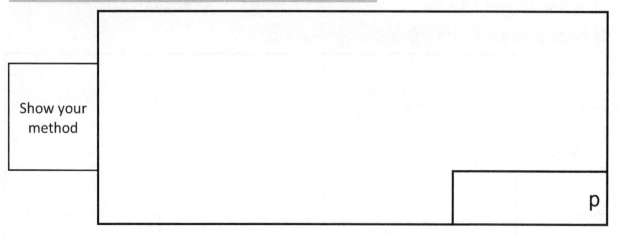

Show your method

p

2 marks

10 Last year, Michael went to three different zoos.
Two of his tickets cost £12 each.
The other ticket cost £15.75.

What was the **mean average** cost of the tickets?

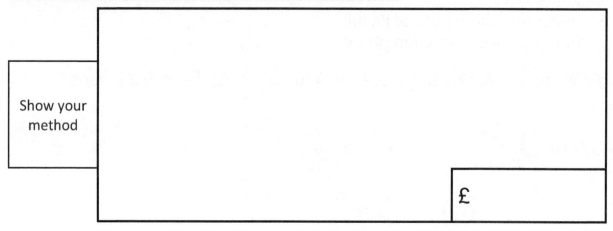

Show your method

£

2 marks

11 Complete each sentence.

a) There are ⬚ grams in **half a kilogram**.

1 mark

b) There are ⬚ millilitres in **one litre**.

1 mark

12 Here is a number pyramid.

The number in any box is the **product** of the two numbers below it.

Fill in the missing numbers.

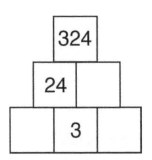

3 marks

13 Kazim is making a tower of wooden blocks.

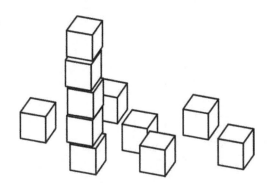

Each block is 6.5 cm tall.
The tower he makes is 110.5 cm tall.

How many blocks are there in the tower?

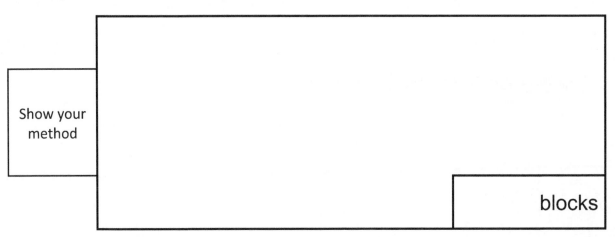

Show your
method

blocks

2 marks

14 This is the net of a cube.

What is the volume of the cube?

cm³

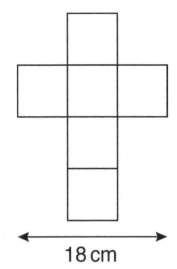

18 cm

1 mark

15 A square has an area of 16 cm².

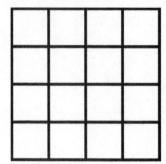

a) Draw a rectangle with the same area.

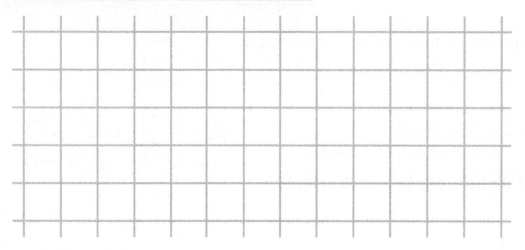

1 mark

b) Draw a triangle with the same area.

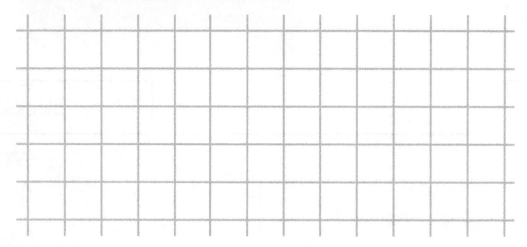

1 mark

16 The prologue, contents and other pages in Oscar's book make up 12 pages in total.

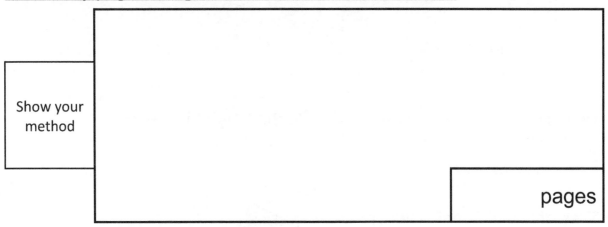

On Monday Oscar read $\frac{3}{7}$ of the story pages of his book.

By Friday he had read the **remaining** 88 pages of the story.

How many pages **altogether** are there in Oscar's book?

Show your method

pages

3 marks

17 Calculate the area of this parallelogram.

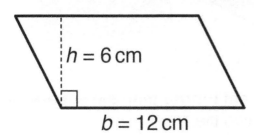

$h = 6\,\text{cm}$

$b = 12\,\text{cm}$

cm²

1 mark

18 Here are two similar shapes.

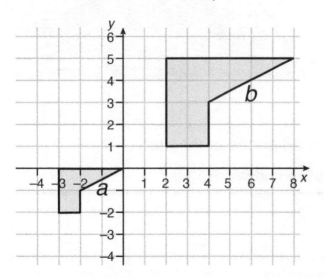

Write the ratio of the length of side *a* to the length of side *b*.

a : *b* = [   ]

1 mark

19 Tiles of two different sizes are
used in a kitchen.

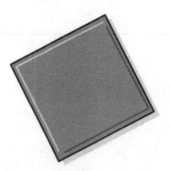 

The square tiles measure 8 cm by 8 cm.
The rectangular tiles are 5 cm **shorter** and 2 cm **longer** than the square tiles.
What is the **difference in area** between the two tiles?

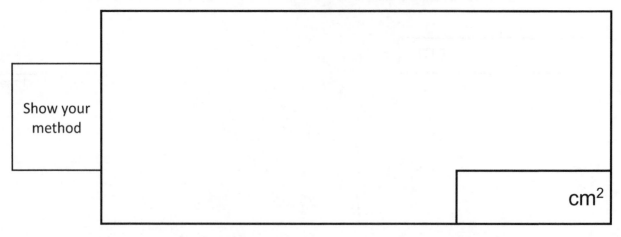

Show your
method

cm²

3 marks

Total marks ………/35

1 $9 \times 7 \times 5 =$

1 mark

2 $96 \div 8 =$

1 mark

3 $9,042 - 579 =$

1 mark

4 $56 - 9.6 =$

1 mark

5 $80.5 \times 1,000 =$

1 mark

6 $9^2 - 15 =$

1 mark

7 $34,906 + 23,097 =$

1 mark

8 $27.09 - 9.88 =$

1 mark

9 $4\frac{1}{3} \times 9 =$

1 mark

10 $1.07 \div 100 =$

1 mark

11 $5.987 + 549.65 =$

1 mark

12 $60.02 \times 100 =$

1 mark

13 $99 - 6 \times 8 =$

1 mark

14 35% of $1500 =$

1 mark

15 $2\frac{5}{6} - \frac{4}{9} =$

1 mark

16 $5.08 \times 150 =$

1 mark

17 $\frac{5}{8} \div 10 =$

1 mark

18

$$3\ 7\ \overline{)6\ 9\ 4\ 5}$$

Show your method   2 marks

19 $\frac{5}{6} \times \frac{2}{3} =$

1 mark

20   60% of 1400 =

1 mark

21 $\frac{9}{12} + 5\frac{1}{6} =$

1 mark

22 $\frac{3}{7} \times \frac{3}{9} =$

1 mark

23 $\frac{3}{7} \div 5 =$

1 mark

24

```
      7 0 4 0
  ×       7 7
```

Show your method   2 marks

25 $69 - 7 \times 8 =$

1 mark

26 $4.05 \times 22 =$

1 mark

27 $0.07 \div 10 =$

1 mark

28 $\frac{8}{9} \times \frac{7}{8} =$

1 mark

29 66% of $275 =$

1 mark

30 9.78×260

1 mark

31 $8\frac{4}{5} - 6\frac{2}{3} =$

1 mark

32

```
        9 0 0 8
    ×         4 9
```

Show your method   2 marks

33

```
  4 8 3 0 7 8
```

Show your method   2 marks

34 $3,000,000 +$ [   ] $+ 4,000 = 3,064,000$

1 mark

35 $10{,}000{,}000 +$ ☐ $+ 5{,}000 = 15{,}005{,}000$

1 mark

36 $50{,}000{,}000 + 400{,}000 + 6{,}000 + 90 =$

1 mark

Total marks ..../40

1 This graph shows the favourite fruit of each child in a school.

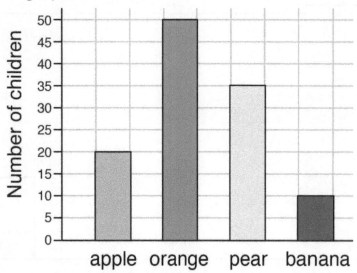

a) Which fruit is the most popular?

_____

b) How many more children liked pear than banana?

_____

2 Here is a shape on a grid.
Complete the design so that it is symmetrical about the mirror line.
Use a ruler to draw the lines.

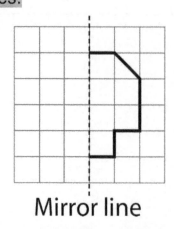

Mirror line

3 What number is halfway between 3.7 and 4.9?

_____

4 Vicky is making up bags of sweets for a party.
The bags have sweets of two different colours inside.

There are four colours of sweet to choose from:
yellow, purple, green and **orange**.

Write the **three** missing combinations.

The bags could contain sweets of
these colours:

* yellow and purple

* yellow and green

* yellow and orange

* _____ and _____

* _____ and _____

* _____ and _____

_____
2 marks

5 Hattie is saving up for a new bicycle.

The bicycle costs £110.50.
So far she has saved £68.95.

How much **more** money does she
need to save?

£ [   ]

_____
1 mark

6 Here is a triangle.

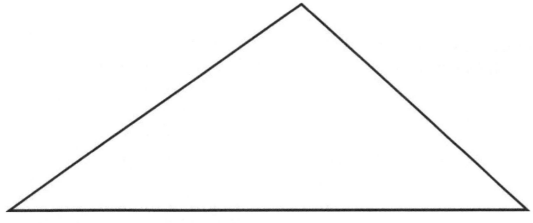

Measure the largest angle.

[   ] °

_____
1 mark

7   Five people gave money to charity.

Three of them each gave £10.
Another one gave £7.50.
The fifth person gave £2.25 more than
the one who gave the least.

How much did the fifth person give?

_____

1 mark

What was the mean amount given to charity?

Show your
method

£

2 marks

8   Complete the boxes.

5 miles = [   ] km

[   ] miles = 40 km

2 marks

9   Join dots on the grid to make a
quadrilateral with exactly two
right angles.

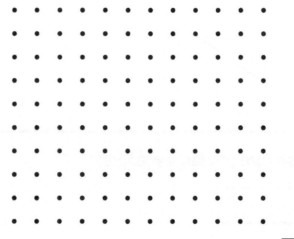

1 mark

10 Two of the angles in a triangle are 80° and 20°.
Harry says:

> It is an isosceles triangle.

Explain why Harry is correct.

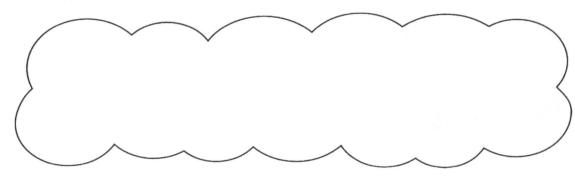

2 marks

11 40 adults and 80 children were asked which kind of pizza they like best.
These two pie charts show the results.

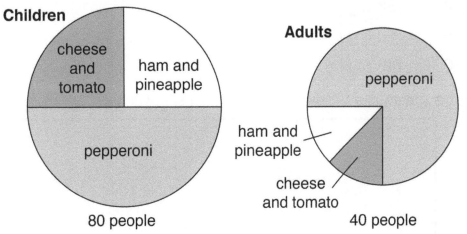

Children

cheese and tomato
ham and pineapple
pepperoni

80 people

Adults

pepperoni
ham and pineapple
cheese and tomato

40 people

Mairi says:

> The pie charts show that more adults than children like pepperoni best.

Mairi is incorrect.

Explain how you know.

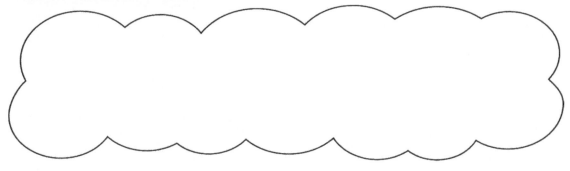

1 mark

12 Fill in the boxes to complete the sentences.

Isosceles triangles have ☐ equal sides.

Equilateral triangles have ☐ equal sides.

Scalene triangles have ☐ equal sides.

2 marks

13 The masses of six books were measured.

Book	Mass
1	89 g
2	115.7 g
3	176.4 g
4	98.5 g
5	100.8 g
6	146.5 g

What is the mean mass of the books?

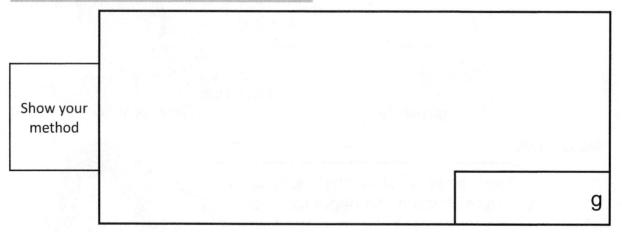

Show your method

g

2 marks

14 Here is a net of a 3D shape.

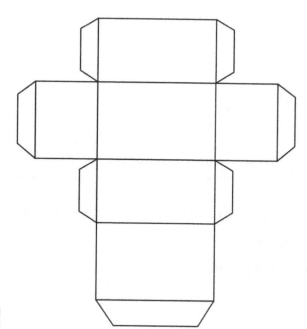

What is the name of the shape?

_____

1 mark

How many faces does the shape have?

_____

1 mark

15 Here is a drawing of a 3D shape.

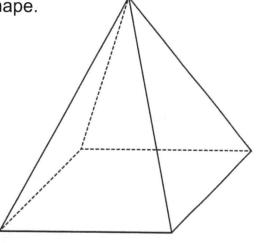

Complete the table.

Number of faces	Number of vertices	Number of edges

2 marks

16

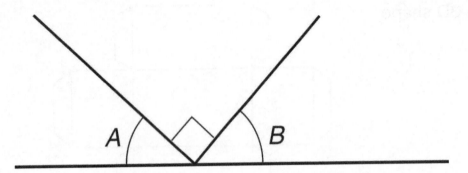

Ashid says: 'All three angles will add up to 200°.'

Is he correct?   Yes / No

Explain your answer.

2 marks

The size of angle *A* is 42°.

What is the size of angle *B*?

_____

1 mark

17 Here are two similar shapes.

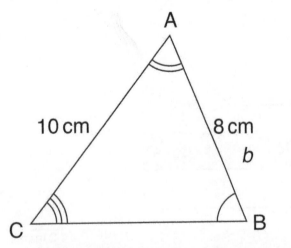

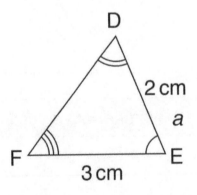

Write the ratio of the length of side *a* to the length of side *b*.

a : *b* = [:   ]

1 mark

18 A tractor wheel has a **radius** of 27 cm.

What is the diameter of the tractor wheel?

cm

1 mark

19 The numbers in this sequence increase by the same amount each time.

Write the missing numbers.

		2	$2\frac{2}{3}$		4

3 marks

20 A group of children were asked what their favourite sport was.

$\frac{4}{9}$ said rugby was their favourite.

$\frac{1}{6}$ said netball was their favourite.

The remaining children said their favourite was **football**.

What fraction of the total number liked football best?

Show your method

2 marks

Total marks ………./35

69

1 $\frac{6}{7} + \frac{9}{7} =$

1 mark

2 $806 \times 7 =$

1 mark

3 $54.8 - 9.94 =$

1 mark

4 $8^3 - 17 =$

1 mark

5 $5,098 - 4,109 =$

1 mark

6 $9^2 - 15 =$

1 mark

7 $\frac{2}{7} + \frac{4}{5} =$

1 mark

8 $3.798 - 1.96 =$

1 mark

9 $3\frac{2}{8} \times 24 =$

1 mark

10 $4,078 + 7,009 =$

1 mark

11 $58 + 99 \div 11 =$

1 mark

12

$$9 \; 9 \; | \; 8 \; 6 \; 4 \; 6$$

Show your method   2 marks

13 $0.007 \times 100 =$

1 mark

14 48% of $300 =$

1 mark

15 $5.67 \times 300 =$

1 mark

16 $4\frac{6}{8} - 2\frac{1}{2} =$

1 mark

17 $\frac{4}{12} \div 9 =$

1 mark

18 $\frac{1}{8} \times \frac{5}{6} =$

1 mark

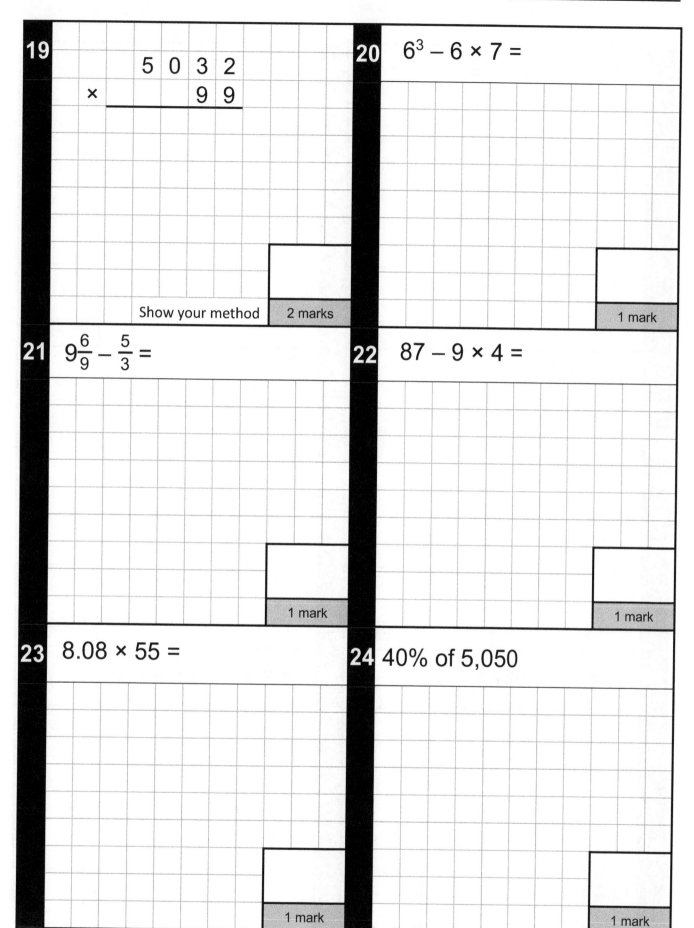

19

$$
\begin{array}{r}
5\ 0\ 3\ 2 \\
\times 9\ 9 \\
\hline
\end{array}
$$

Show your method   2 marks

20 $6^3 - 6 \times 7 =$

1 mark

21 $9\frac{6}{9} - \frac{5}{3} =$

1 mark

22 $87 - 9 \times 4 =$

1 mark

23 $8.08 \times 55 =$

1 mark

24 40% of 5,050

1 mark

Name _____

25 $265 - 12 \times 12 =$

1 mark

26 $45.8 \div 100 =$

1 mark

27 $7\frac{4}{8} + 2\frac{7}{12} =$

1 mark

28 $\frac{2}{7} \times \frac{9}{12} =$

1 mark

29 20% of 1750 =

1 mark

30 $4{,}309 - 108 \div 9 =$

1 mark

31 $9.57 \times 49 =$

1 mark

32 $1.009 \times 100 =$

1 mark

33 $\frac{10}{13} \div 7 =$

1 mark

34 91% of 850

1 mark

35
```
      8 9 0 5
    ×     8 4
    _____
```
Show your method   2 marks

36
```
7 6 | 3 0 2 1
```
Show your method   2 marks

Total marks ………/40

v

1 On the line below, mark the point that is 8.6 centimetres from A.

|
A

2 Mo is running the 10,000 m race.

He has completed $\frac{5}{8}$ of the race.

How many more metres are **left** for Mo to run?

Show your method

m

3 A sweet shop ordered 58 large tubs of sweets.

They ran out of sweets on Tuesday so decided to order $4\frac{1}{2}$ times as many the following week.

How many tubs of sweets did they order the next week?

Show your method

tubs

4 William swam 4 lengths of the pool in 4 minutes 19 seconds.
Jessie swam 4 lengths of the pool in 27 seconds **less** than William.

a) How long did Jessie take?

min	sec

1 mark

Tamzin completed the same 4 lengths 48 seconds **after** William.

b) How long did Tamzin take?

min	sec

1 mark

5 Tick the numbers that are common factors of both **16 and 24**.

2 ☐

4 ☐

5 ☐

8 ☐

12 ☐

2 marks

6 12,306,594

Complete the sentences for the above number.

_____ million

_____ hundred thousand

_____ thousand

_____ hundred

2 marks

7 Kirsty, Rob and Morgan are counting cars that are travelling along a road. They each watch for two hours and count all the cars they see within that time.

Kirsty counts 1,898 cars.
Rob counts 217 **more** cars than Kirsty.
Morgan counts 105 **fewer** cars than Kirsty.

How many cars do they count **altogether**?

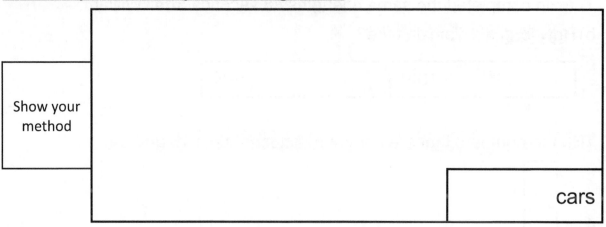

Show your method

cars

3 marks

8 Write the correct symbol in each box to make the statements correct.

> = <

9 × 8 ☐ 11 × 7

150 ÷ 10 ☐ 132 ÷ 12

8 × 12 ☐ 10 × 11

144 ÷ 12 ☐ 4 × 3

2 marks

9   Some friends order two pizzas.

cheese and tomato   pepperoni

Maui eats $\frac{2}{3}$ of a slice of pepperoni pizza and $\frac{1}{2}$ of a slice of cheese and tomato pizza.

What fraction of the **total amount of pizza available** did Maui eat?

Show your method	
	pizza

1 mark

10 There are 25 children in a class. They go on a school trip.
The total cost of the trip is £234.
The total cost is divided equally among all the children.

How much does each child pay?

Show your method	
	£

2 marks

79

11 Here is a parallelogram.

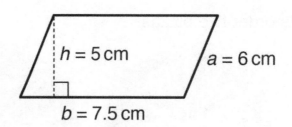

$h = 5\,cm$ $a = 6\,cm$

$b = 7.5\,cm$

a) What is the formula for finding the area?

_____

1 mark

b) What is the area of this parallelogram?

_____

1 mark

12 Car park A holds 12,036 cars.
Car Park B has 15 floors and holds 1,252 cars per floor.

How many more cars does Car Park B hold than Car Park A?

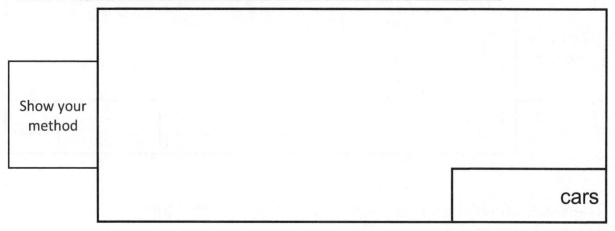

Show your method

cars

3 marks

13 Here is a cuboid.

Kieran says: 'I can work out the volume of this by multiplying the height by the width and doubling it'

Is he correct?   Yes / No

Explain your answer.

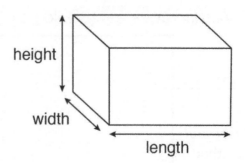

height

width

length

_____

_____

1 mark

14 Harriet has 32 metres of bunting.

She uses $\frac{4}{10}$ to decorate upstairs in her house.

She uses $\frac{1}{8}$ to decorate downstairs in her house.

How many metres does she have left for the outside of the house?

Show your method

m

3 marks

15 Otto buys a cake at a cake sale.

He divides it equally among himself and 4 friends.

What fraction does each person get?

_____

1 mark

16 Emma says that 5 + (6 × 8) = 88.

She is incorrect.

Explain how she should have worked out the answer.

1 mark

17 A school is raising money for its
classes to spend on new equipment.

They raise:
- £460.24 from cake sales
- £1,156.20 from the summer fair
- £112 selling lollies at sports day.

The school shares the money equally among its 14 classes.

How much does each class receive to spend on new equipment?

3 marks

18 This is the net of a cuboid with
two square faces.

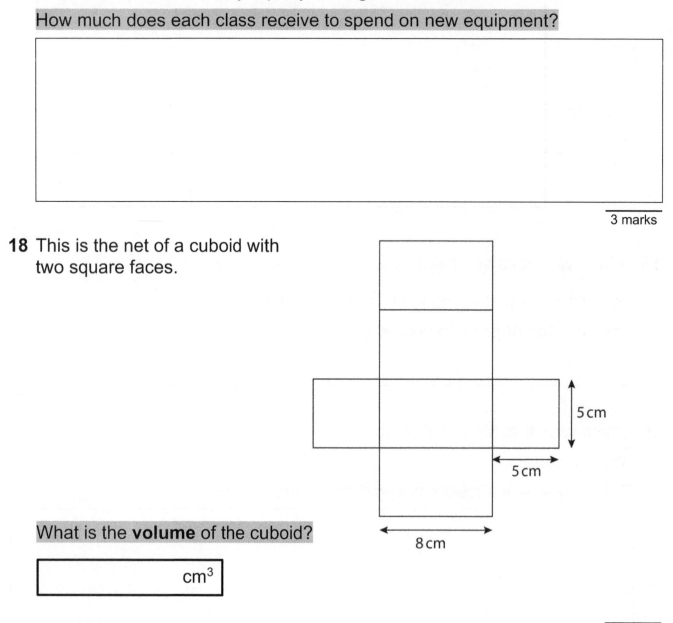

What is the **volume** of the cuboid?

cm³

2 marks

Total marks ………/35

Year 6 Autumn Half Term 1: Arithmetic Mark Scheme

Question	Requirement	Mark	Additional guidance	Level of demand
1	4,567	1		T
2	36	1		T
3	9	1		T
4	$\frac{7}{8}$	1		T
5	900	1		T
6	5,201	1		T
7	376	1		T
8	8.14	1		T
9	64	1		T
10	9	1		T
11	21	1		E
12	15	1		E
13	4,890,000	1		T
14	39.725	1	Also accept remainders shown as fractions, e.g. $\frac{725}{1000}$ or $\frac{29}{40}$	E
15	8	1		T
16	56	1		T
17	$\frac{3}{12}$ or $\frac{1}{3}$	1		T
18	13,999	1		T
19	4,696	1		T
20	5	1		E
21	700	1		T
22	49,000	1		E
23	61.505	2	Also accept rounded to 2 d.p., i.e. 61.51, or a fraction for the remainder $61\frac{1}{2}$	G
24	155	1		E
25	26	1		E
26	78.3	1	Also accept remainders given as a fraction, e.g. $78\frac{3}{10}$	E
27	30,240	2		G
28	443	1		E
29	39,358	1		E
30	42	2		G
31	4,000,000	1		E
32	4,000	1		E

Year 6 Autumn Half Term 1: Arithmetic Mark Scheme

Threshold scores
Working towards the expected standard: 0–20
Working at the expected standard: 21–27
Working at greater depth: 28–35

Balance of difficulty of questions in the paper
17 marks at working towards (T)
12 marks at the expected standard (E)
6 marks at working at greater depth (G)

Year 6 Autumn Half Term 1: Reasoning Mark Scheme

Question	Requirement	Mark	Additional guidance	Level of demand
1	787	1		T
2	181 − 28 = 153 OR 181 − 153 = 28	1		T
3	£213	2	**1 mark** for correct addition calculation with an answer of £637.	T
4	Missing numbers are 9, 6 and 42	1	<table><tr><td>x</td><td>9</td><td>6</td></tr><tr><td>9</td><td>81</td><td>54</td></tr><tr><td>7</td><td>63</td><td>42</td></tr></table>	T
5	Boxes ticked should be: 2, 3, 5, 7, 13, 17, 19	1		E
6	add 65 then subtract 2 AND add 60 then add 3	2	**1 mark** for each correct answer.	T
7	D E B A C	1		T
8	679,080	1		T
9	Children should draw a number line with −4 marked with a jump to 0 with a +4 or a jump back from 0 marked −4 and then a marking of 23 and a jump from 0 marked +23 or back from 23 to 0 with a marking of −23. They should have an answer of 27 °C.	2	**1 mark** for correctly drawn and labelled number line. **1 mark** for correct answer in the box of 27°C.	E
10	1990	1		T
11	Total of all items = £34.56 Change she receives = £1.44 or 144p	2	**1 mark** for correct addition of items.	E
12	2,156,800 2,160,000 2,000,000	2	**1 mark** for two correct responses.	E
13	Explanation should show that although Sam bought double the number of packs he has 48 cups (as there were fewer cups in each pack). Mika has 36 cups.	1	Accept explanations that make reference to: • Different number of cups in each pack • 48 is double 24, whereas double 36 is 72.	E
14	3, 6, 15	2	**1 mark** for two correct answers.	E
15	Any three numbers that have digit totals of 20 and no repeating digits between the two numbers given, e.g. 128,630	2	Accept any answer where the digits total 20 and are not repeated, e.g. 126,803 126,830 134,507	G
16	Explanation that shows that 5,712 can be made by adding 408 to 13 x 408	1	Explanation needs to show clear method. The answer **does not** need to be given for award of the mark if the explanation is clear.	G
17	24 g	2	**1 mark** for correct method.	E
18	> < < >	2	**1 mark** for three correct answers.	E

| 19 | White House area = 1,326 square metres. Buckingham Palace is 11,634 square metres bigger. | 3 | Award **3 marks** for correct answer. If incorrect, award **2 marks** for correct identification of White House area as 1,326 metres. Award **1 mark** for evidence of an appropriate method which contains more than **one** arithmetical error. | G |

Threshold scores
Working towards the expected standard: 0–17
Working at the expected standard: 18–23
Working at greater depth: 24–30

Balance of difficulty of questions in the paper
10 marks at working towards (T)
14 marks at the expected standard (E)
6 marks at working at greater depth (G)

Year 6 Autumn Half Term 2: Arithmetic Mark Scheme

Question	Requirement	Mark	Additional guidance	Level of demand
1	1,170	1	Accept 1170 without the comma.	T
2	14.1	1	Do not accept a mixed number – it must be written in decimal form.	T
3	54,217	1	Also accept 54 217 without the comma.	T
4	297.33	1	Also accept remainder given as a fraction, $297\frac{1}{3}$ and the decimal being shown as a recurring decimal.	T
5	46.546	1	Must be written in decimal form.	T
6	51,200	1	Accept 51 200 written without the comma.	T
7	55.095	1	Must be written in decimal form.	T
8	$\frac{19}{100}$	1		T
9	7,999,993	1	Accept 7 999 993 written without commas.	E
10	2,596,109	1	Accept 2 596 109 written without commas.	E
11	78	1		E
12	66	1		T
13	6,479,520	1	Accept 6 479 520 written without commas.	E
14	6,471	1		T
15	25	1		T
16	$\frac{4}{20}$	1	Also accept in its lowest form of $\frac{1}{5}$. Do not accept decimals.	E
17	$\frac{1}{8}$	1	Accept equivalent fractions or an **exact** decimal equivalent, e.g. 0.125.	E
18	488	1		E
19	8.344	1		T
20	108	1		E
21	$\frac{52}{15}$ or $3\frac{7}{15}$	1	Accept equivalent mixed numbers, fractions or the decimal equivalent, e.g. 3.466 666 (accept any unambiguous indications of the recurring digit).	E
22	26	1		E
23	$\frac{12}{20}$	1	Accept equivalent fractions or an **exact** decimal equivalent, e.g. $\frac{6}{10}$ or 0.6.	T
24	18	1		E
25	$\frac{1}{4}$	1	Accept equivalent fractions or an **exact** decimal equivalent, e.g. $\frac{6}{24}$ or 0.25.	E
26	$\frac{3}{16}$	1	Accept equivalent fractions or an **exact** decimal equivalent, e.g. 0.1875.	E
27	$\frac{29}{24}$ or $1\frac{5}{24}$	1		G

Year 6 Autumn Half Term 2: Arithmetic Mark Scheme

28	$4\frac{3}{20}$ or $\frac{83}{20}$	1	Accept equivalent mixed numbers, fractions or an **exact** decimal equivalent, e.g. 4.15.	G
29	45	2	Award **2 marks** for the correct answer of **45**. If the answer is incorrect, award **1 mark** for a formal method of division with no more than 1 arithmetic error.	G
30	126,944	2	Award **2 marks** for the correct answer of **126,944**. If the answer is incorrect, award **1 mark** for a formal method of long multiplication with no more than 1 arithmetic error.	G
31	83	2	Award **2 marks** for the correct answer of **83**. If the answer is incorrect, award **1 mark** for a formal method of division with no more than **one** arithmetical error.	G
32	100,000	1	Accept 100 000 written without the comma.	E

Threshold scores
Working towards the expected standard: 20 or fewer
Working at the expected standard: 21–27
Working at greater depth: 28–35

Balance of difficulty of questions in the paper
13 marks at working towards (T)
14 marks at the expected standard (E)
8 marks at working at greater depth (G)

Year 6 Autumn Half Term 2: Reasoning Mark Scheme

Question	Requirement	Mark	Additional guidance	Level of demand
1	Both values correct as shown. $\dfrac{1}{3} = \dfrac{3}{9} = \dfrac{6}{18}$	1	Both values must be correct for the award of **1 mark**.	T
2	84 × 5 **or** 45 × 8 **or** 48 × 5 **or** 85 × 4	1		T
3	3,600 eggs	2	Award **2 marks** for the correct answer of 3,600. If the answer is incorrect, award **1 mark** for evidence of appropriate complete method with no more than one arithmetic error. Do **not** accept sight of a correct multiplication for **1 mark** unless part of the calculation is completed correctly. Misreads are **not** allowed.	T
4	5,739	1		T
5	0.972	1		T
6	40%	1		T
7	50p	2	Award **2 marks** for the correct answer of 50p. If the answer is incorrect, award 1 mark for evidence of appropriate complete method with no more than one arithmetic error. Do **not** accept sight of a correct division for one mark unless part of the calculation is completed correctly. Misreads are **not** allowed.	E
8	$\dfrac{29}{48}$	2	Award 2 marks for the correct answer of $\dfrac{29}{48}$. If the answer is incorrect, award **1 mark** for evidence of an appropriate method. Accept equivalent fractions, e.g. $\dfrac{58}{96}$. Answer needs to be obtained for the award of **1 mark**.	E
9	$\dfrac{3}{9} = \dfrac{6}{18} = \dfrac{2}{6}$	1 1		E
10	Second box only ticked.	1	Accept alternative unambiguous positive indication of the correct answer, e.g. Y.	E
11	15 **and** 30 **and** 45 only	1	Numbers may be given in any order.	E
12	Award two marks for all four rows completed correctly as shown. $3\frac{3}{4}$ — 3.6 $3\frac{1}{3}$ — 3.25 $3\frac{19}{100}$ — 3.2 $3\frac{6}{7}$ — 3.7	2	Accept alternative unambiguous positive indications of the correct numbers, e.g. numbers ticked. If the answer is incorrect, award **1 mark** for three rows completed correctly.	E

Year 6 Autumn Half Term 2: Reasoning Mark Scheme

13	Triangle with vertices at (−4, −5) and (−2, −2) and (0, −5) drawn on the grid as shown.	1	Accept slight inaccuracies in drawing.	E
14	Award 2 marks for numbers completed, as shown. 3558.3 355,830 3558.3	2	Award **1 mark** for any two numbers completed correctly. **Do not** accept transcription errors or misreads for this question.	E
15	£49.32	3	Award **3 marks** for the correct answer of £49.32. If the answer is incorrect, award **2 marks** for evidence of an appropriate complete method with no more than one arithmetic error. Award **1 mark** for evidence of an appropriate complete method.	G
16	> > = <	2	Award **2 marks** for all symbols correct, as shown. Award **1 mark** for any three symbols correct.	E
17	279 m²	3	Award **3 marks** for the correct answer of 279 m². If the answer is incorrect, award 2 marks for sight of 117 as evidence of 13 × 9 completed correctly or evidence of an appropriate method with no more than one arithmetic error. Award **1 mark** for evidence of an appropriate method. Answer need not be obtained for the award of **1 mark**. A misread of a number may affect the award of marks. No marks are awarded if there is more than one misread or if the mathematics is simplified.	G
18	(9, −1) (5, −6)	1 1	Accept unambiguous answers written on the diagram.	G

Threshold scores
Working towards the expected standard: 17 or fewer
Working at the expected standard: 18–23
Working at greater depth: 24–30

Balance of difficulty of questions in the paper
7 marks at working towards (T)
15 marks at the expected standard (E)
8 marks at working at greater depth (G)

© HarperCollins*Publishers* Ltd 2019

90

Year 6 Spring Half Term 1: Arithmetic Mark Scheme

Question	Requirement	Mark	Additional guidance	Level of demand
1	$\dfrac{5}{12}$	1	Accept equivalent fractions or decimal equivalent, e.g. 0.416 (accept any unambiguous indication of the recurring digits).	T
2	578	1		T
3	2,892	1	Also accept 2892 written without commas.	T
4	7,406	1	Also accept 7406 written without commas.	T
5	$\dfrac{11}{9}$ or $1\dfrac{2}{9}$	1	Accept equivalent mixed numbers, fractions or decimal equivalent, e.g. 1.22 (accept any unambiguous indication of the recurring digit).	T
6	$\dfrac{3}{8}$	1	Accept equivalent fractions or **exact** decimal equivalent, e.g. 0.375.	T
7	$\dfrac{63}{2}$	1	Accept equivalent fractions or an exact decimal equivalent, e.g. $\dfrac{252}{8}$ or 31.5	T
8	4	1		T
9	3.166	1		T
10	$\dfrac{23}{18}$ or $1\dfrac{5}{18}$	1	Accept equivalent mixed numbers, fractions or decimal equivalent, e.g. 1.277 (accept any unambiguous indication of the recurring digit).	T
11	15.65	1		T
12	65	1		E
13	195	1	Do **not** accept 195%.	E
14	134	1		E
15	$\dfrac{2}{28}$ or $\dfrac{1}{14}$	1	Accept equivalent fractions or decimal equivalent, e.g. 0.071 428 5.	E
16	$4\dfrac{3}{5}$ or $\dfrac{23}{5}$	1	Accept equivalent fractions or mixed numbers.	E
17	120	1		E
18	13.92	1		E
19	$\dfrac{3}{60}$ or $\dfrac{1}{20}$	1	Accept equivalent fractions or an **exact** decimal equivalent, e.g. 0.05.	E
20	0.0095	1		E
21	$\dfrac{1}{8}$	1	Accept equivalent fractions or an **exact** decimal equivalent, e.g. 0.125.	E
22	44.45	1		E
23	220	1		E
24	$\dfrac{68}{9}$ or $7\dfrac{5}{9}$	1	Accept equivalent fractions or mixed numbers.	E
25	$\dfrac{6}{35}$	1	Accept equivalent fractions.	E
26	60	1		E
27	0.04	1		E
28	$\dfrac{37}{14}$ or $2\dfrac{9}{14}$	1	Accept equivalent fractions or mixed numbers.	G

29	42.54	1		E
30	594	1		E
31	60.5	2	Award **2 marks** for the correct answer of **60.5**. If the answer is incorrect, award **1 mark** for a formal method of division with no more than 1 arithmetic error.	G
32	338,688	2	Award **2 marks** for the correct answer of 338,688. If the answer is incorrect, award **1 mark** for a formal method of long multiplication with no more than 1 arithmetic error.	G
33	41.25	2	Award **2 marks** for the correct answer of 41.25. If the answer is incorrect, award **1 mark** for a formal method of division with no more than 1 arithmetic error.	G
34	243,825	2	Award **2 marks** for the correct answer of 243,825. If the answer is incorrect, award **1 mark** for a formal method of long multiplication with no more than 1 arithmetic error.	G
35	1,000,000	1	Accept 1 000 000 written without commas.	E
36	80,000	1	Accept 80 000 written without commas.	E

Threshold scores

Working towards the expected standard: 23 or fewer
Working at the expected standard: 24–31
Working at greater depth: 32–40

Balance of difficulty of questions in the paper
11 marks at working towards (T)
20 marks at the expected standard (E)
9 marks at working at greater depth (G)

Year 6 Spring Half Term 1: Reasoning Mark Scheme

Question	Requirement	Mark	Additional guidance	Level of demand
1	2.6	2	Award **2 marks** for the correct answer. If the answer is incorrect, award **1 mark** for evidence of an appropriate method. Answer need not be obtained for the award of **1 mark**.	T
2	6 squares to the left 5 squares up	1		T
3	prime numbers factors of 50 even numbers 11 17 5 25 10 20 32	3	Award **3** marks for all seven numbers placed correctly as shown. If the answer is incorrect, award **2 marks** for six numbers placed correctly. Award **1 mark** for five numbers placed correctly.	T
4	Two numbers circled: 0.125 **and** 0.545.	1	Accept alternative unambiguous positive indications, e.g. numbers ticked or underlined.	T
5	Numbers in order, as shown. 2.005 1.564 1.456 0.987 0.789	1		T
6a 6b	8 −6.5	1 1	**Do not** accept −8 or 8−. **Do not** accept 6.5−.	E
7	16,465,801	1	Also accept 16 465 801 written without commas.	E
8	£192.50	2	Award **2 marks** for the correct answer of £192.50. If the answer is incorrect, award **1 mark** for evidence of an appropriate method.	E
9	red and green red and blue green and blue	2	Award **2 marks** for the correct answers. If the answer is incorrect, award **1 mark** for **two** correct combinations.	E
10	Fractions written in the correct order, as shown: $\frac{2}{7}, \frac{3}{4}, \frac{5}{2}$	1	Accept the fraction joined to the correct box, rather than written in it.	E
11a 11b	$6n + 22 = 76$ or $n = (76 − 22) ÷ 6$ 9	1 1		G E
12	Star = 17p Triangle = 20p	1 1		G
13a 13b 13c	54% $\frac{6}{25}$ 0.22	1 1 1		E
14	1,807 180,700 27.8	2	Award **1 mark** for any two numbers completed correctly.	E
15a 15b	£1.26 17	1 2	Award **2 marks** for the correct answer. If the answer is incorrect, award **1 mark** for evidence of an appropriate method. Answer need not be obtained for the award of **1 mark**.	G

Year 6 Spring Half Term 1: Reasoning Mark Scheme

16	$\dfrac{1}{6}$ 0.333 0.833	2	Award **1 mark** for any two boxes completed correctly.	G
17	$\dfrac{7}{8}$ Explanation showing that $\dfrac{9}{12}$ = 0.75	1 1		E
18	83 s = 7	1 1		E
19	£27	1		E

Threshold scores
Working towards the expected standard: 20 or fewer
Working at the expected standard: 21–27
Working at greater depth: 28–35

Balance of difficulty of questions in the paper
8 marks at working towards (T)
19 marks at the expected standard (E)
8 marks at working at greater depth (G)

Year 6 Spring Half Term 2: Arithmetic Mark Scheme

Question	Requirement	Mark	Additional guidance	Level of demand
1	5,598	1	Accept 5598 written without commas.	T
2	2,983	1	Accept 2983 written without commas.	T
3	162	1		T
4	3,924	1	Accept 3924 written without commas.	T
5	125	1		T
6	$\frac{98}{5}$	1	Accept equivalent fractions or **exact** decimal equivalent, e.g. 19.6.	T
7	69	1		T
8	110.64	1		T
9	638,695	1	Accept 638 695 written without commas.	T
10	$\frac{14}{24}$	1	Accept equivalent mixed numbers, fractions or an **exact** decimal equivalent, e.g. $\frac{7}{12}$ or 0.5833 (accept any unambiguous indication of the recurring digit).	T
11	12 or $\frac{120}{10}$	1	Accept equivalent fractions.	T
12	79	1		E
13	420	1		E
14	49.5	1		E
15	$\frac{10}{56}$	1		E
16	40	1		E
17	36	1		E
18	0.004	1		E
19	$\frac{113}{12}$ or $9\frac{5}{12}$	1	Accept equivalent mixed numbers, fractions or an **exact** decimal equivalent, e.g. 9.4166 (accept any unambiguous indication of the recurring digit).	E
20	504	1		E
21	$\frac{6}{32}$	1	Accept equivalent fractions or an **exact** decimal equivalent, e.g. 0.1875	E
22	145	1		E
23	$\frac{5}{45}$ or $\frac{1}{9}$	1	Accept equivalent fractions or an **exact** decimal equivalent, e.g. 0.111 (accept any unambiguous indication of the recurring digit).	E
24	$\frac{43}{8}$ or $5\frac{3}{8}$	1	Accept equivalent mixed numbers, fractions or an **exact** decimal equivalent, e.g. 5.375.	E
25	456.95	1		G
26	1,320	1		E
27	$\frac{6}{91}$	1	Accept equivalent fractions or a decimal equivalent, e.g. 0.065 934.	E
28	41	1		E

Year 6 Spring Half Term 2: Arithmetic Mark Scheme

29	1,260	1		E
30	158,620	2	Award **2 marks** for the correct answer of **158,620**. If the answer is incorrect, award **1 mark** for a formal method of long multiplication with no more than one arithmetic error.	G
31	23.5	2	Award **2 marks** for the correct answer of **23.5**. If the answer is incorrect, award **1 mark** for a formal method of division with no more than one arithmetical error.	G
32	642,972	2	Award **2 marks** for the correct answer of **642,972**. If the answer is incorrect, award **1 mark** for a formal method of long multiplication with no more than one arithmetical error.	G
33	24.25	2	Award **2 marks** for the correct answer of **24.25**. If the answer is incorrect, award **1 mark** for a formal method of division with no more than one arithmetical error.	G
34	56	1		E
35	7,000	1		E
36	12,000,000	1	Accept 12 000 000 written without commas.	E

Threshold scores

Working towards the expected standard: 23 or fewer
Working at the expected standard: 24–31
Working at greater depth: 32–40

Balance of difficulty of questions in the paper
11 marks at working towards (T)
20 marks at the expected standard (E)
9 marks working at greater depth (G)

Year 6 Spring Half Term 2: Reasoning Mark Scheme

Question	Requirement	Mark	Additional guidance	Level of demand
1	7 5 15	2	Award **1 mark** if two boxes are completed correctly.	T
2	15.15	1	Award the mark for unambiguous positive indication of the box e.g. circled, underlined.	T
3	C	1	Award the mark for unambiguous positive indication of the cuboid e.g. circled, underlined.	T
4	0.06 **and** 0.79	1	Award the mark for unambiguous positive indication of both decimals e.g. ticked, underlined.	T
5	8 cm	2	Award **1 mark** for evidence of a correct method even if the answer is incorrect.	E
6	£1	2	Award **2 marks** for the correct answer of £1. If incorrect, award **1 mark** for evidence of a correct method with no more than one arithmetic error.	T
7	27	2	Award **2 marks** for the correct answer of 27. If incorrect, award **1 mark** for evidence of a correct method with no more than one arithmetic error.	T
8	13.5 cm	2	Award **2 marks** for the correct answer of 13.5 cm. If incorrect, award **1 mark** for evidence of a correct method with no more than one arithmetic error.	E
9	0.6p	2	Award **2 marks** for the correct answer of 0.6p. If incorrect, award **1 mark** for evidence of a correct method with no more than one arithmetic error.	E
10	£13.25	2	Award **2 marks** for the correct answer of £13.25. If incorrect, award **1 mark** for evidence of a correct method with no more than one arithmetic error.	E
11a 11b	500 1000	1 1		E
12	13.5 and 8 **and** 4.5	3	Award **3 marks** for the all three boxes correct. Award **2 marks** for two boxes correct. Award **1 mark** for one box correct.	E
13	17 blocks	2	Award **2 marks** for the correct answer of 17 blocks. If incorrect, award **1 mark** for evidence of a correct method with no more than one arithmetic error.	E
14	216 cm^3	1		E
15a 15b	Shapes drawn with the correct areas.	1 1	Award **1 mark** for each shape drawn with the correct area. Accept small errors with drawing that do not alter the area of the shape.	E G
16	166 pages	3	Award **3 marks** for the correct answer of 166 pages. If incorrect, award **2 marks** for evidence of a correct method but an incorrect answer. Award **1 mark** for evidence of a correct method but no answer reached.	G
17	72 cm^2	1		E
18	1 : 2	1		E

| 19 | 34 cm^2 | | 3 | Award **3 marks** for the correct answer of 34 cm^2. If incorrect, award **2 marks** for evidence of a correct method but an incorrect answer. Award **1 mark** for evidence of a correct method but no answer reached. | G |

Threshold scores

Working towards the expected standard: 20 or
Working at the expected standard: 21–27
Working at greater depth: 28–35

Balance of difficulty of questions in the paper

9 marks at working towards (T)
19 marks at the expected standard (E)
7 marks at working at greater depth (G)

Year 6 Summer Half Term 1: Arithmetic Mark Scheme

Question	Requirement	Mark	Additional guidance	Level of demand
1	315	1		T
2	12	1		T
3	8,463	1	Accept 8463 written without commas.	T
4	46.4	1		T
5	80,500	1	Also accept 80 500 written without commas.	T
6	66	1		T
7	58,003	1		T
8	17.21	1		T
9	39	1		T
10	0.0107	1		T
11	555.637	1		T
12	6,002	1		E
13	51	1		E
14	525	1		E
15	$\frac{43}{18}$	1	Accept equivalent mixed numbers ($2\frac{7}{18}$), fractions or decimal equivalent (2.3888) (accept any unambiguous indication of the recurring digit).	E
16	762	1		E
17	$\frac{1}{16}$	1	Accept equivalent fractions or an **exact** decimal equivalent, e.g. 0.0625.	E
18	187.7027	2	Award **2 marks** for the correct answer of **187.7027**. If the answer is incorrect, award **1 mark** for a formal method of division with no more than one arithmetic error.	G
19	$\frac{5}{9}$	1	Accept equivalent fractions or decimal equivalent, e.g. 0.55 (accept any unambiguous indication of the recurring digit).	E
20	840	1		E
21	$5\frac{11}{12}$ or $\frac{71}{12}$	1	Accept equivalent mixed numbers, fractions or decimal equivalent, e.g. 5.9166 (accept any unambiguous indication of the recurring digit).	E
22	$\frac{1}{7}$	1	Accept equivalent fractions.	E
23	$\frac{3}{35}$	1	Accept equivalent fractions or decimal equivalent, e.g. 0.085 714 285… (accept any unambiguous indication of the recurring digits).	E
24	542,080	2	Award **2 marks** for the correct answer of **542,080**. If the answer is incorrect, award **1 mark** for a formal method of long multiplication with no more than one arithmetic error.	G
25	13	1		E
26	89.1	1		E

27	0.007	1		E
28	$\dfrac{7}{9}$	1	Accept equivalent fractions or decimal equivalent, e.g. 0.77 (accept any unambiguous indication of the recurring digit).	E
29	181.5	1	Also accept $181\dfrac{1}{2}$ written as a mixed number.	G
30	2,542.8	1		G
31	$2\dfrac{2}{15}$ or $\dfrac{32}{15}$	1	Accept equivalent mixed numbers, fractions or decimal equivalent, e.g. 2.133 (accept any unambiguous indication of the recurring digit).	G
32	441,392	2	Award **2 marks** for the correct answer of **441,392**. If the answer is incorrect, award **1 mark** for a formal method of long multiplication with no more than 1 arithmetic error.	G
33	64.125	2	Award **2 marks** for the correct answer of **64.125**. If the answer is incorrect, award **1 mark** for a formal method of division with no more than one arithmetic error.	G
34	60,000	1	Accept 60 000 written without commas.	E
35	5,000,000	1	Accept 5 000 000 written without commas.	E
36	50,406,090	1	Accept 50 406 090 written without commas.	E

Threshold scores

Working towards the expected standard: 23 or fewer
Working at the expected standard: 24–31
Working at greater depth: 32–40

Balance of difficulty of questions in the paper

11 marks at working towards (T)
18 marks at the expected standard (E)
11 marks at working at greater depth (G)

Year 6 Summer Half Term 1: Reasoning Mark Scheme

Question	Requirement	Mark	Additional guidance	Level of demand
1a	orange	1		T
1b	25 children	1		
2		1	Accept slight inaccuracies with drawing if it does not change the image significantly.	T
3	4.3	1		T
4	purple and green purple and orange green and orange	2	Award **2 marks** for three correct combinations written. Award **1 mark** for two correct. Spelling does not need to be correct for the award of the marks.	T
5	£41.55	1		T
6	105°	1		T
7	£9.75 £9.45	1 2	Award **1 mark** for the correct answer of £9.75. Award **2 marks** for the correct answer of £9.45. If incorrect, award **1 mark** for evidence of a correct method with no more than one error.	E
8	8 25	2		E
9	For example: 	1	Accept slight inaccuracies with drawing if it does not change the four sides and angles.	E
10	Explanation should state that isosceles triangles have two angles the same (**1 mark**) and then show that 180 − 20 = 160, 160 divided by 2 is 80 so the missing angle is also 80 (**1 mark**).	2	Accept also 180 − 20 = 160, 160 − 80 = 80.	E
11	Explanation should show that $\frac{1}{2}$ of 80 = 40 $\frac{3}{4}$ of 40 = 30 so she is incorrect	1		E
12	All three boxes completed correctly. 2 3 0	2	Award **2 marks** for all three boxes completed correctly. Award **1 mark** for **two** boxes completed correctly.	E
13	121.15 g	2	Award **2 marks** for the correct answer of 121.15 g. If incorrect, award **1 mark** for evidence of a correct method with only one error.	E
14	cuboid 6	1 1		E
15	Faces = 5 Vertices = 5 Edges = 8	2	If incorrect, award **1 mark** for two boxes completed correctly.	E

16a	No circled with explanation that identifies the total angles on a straight line add up to 180°	2	The marks can be awarded even if no answer is circled if the explanation is correct. If explanation is incorrect, award **1 mark** for correctly circling 'no'.	G G
16b	48°	1		
17	1 : 4	1	Accept 2 : 8	E
18	54 cm	1		E
19	$\dfrac{2}{3}$ $1\dfrac{1}{3}$ or $1\dfrac{2}{6}$ $3\dfrac{1}{3}$ or $3\dfrac{2}{6}$	3	Award **1 mark** for each correctly completed box up to a maximum of **3 marks**.	G
20	$\dfrac{7}{18}$	2	Award **2 marks** for the correct answer of $\dfrac{7}{18}$. If incorrect, award **1 mark** for evidence of a correct method with only one error.	G

Threshold scores
Working towards the expected standard: 20 or fewer
Working at the expected standard: 21–27
Working at greater depth: 28–35

Balance of difficulty of questions in the paper
8 marks at working towards (T)
19 marks at the expected standard (E)
8 marks at working at greater depth (G)

Year 6 Summer Half Term 2: Arithmetic Mark Scheme

Question	Requirement	Mark	Additional guidance	Level of demand
1	$\frac{15}{7}$ or $2\frac{1}{7}$	1	Accept equivalent fractions.	T
2	5,642	1	Accept 5642 written without commas.	T
3	44.86	1		T
4	495	1		T
5	989	1		T
6	66	1		T
7	$1\frac{3}{35}$ or $\frac{38}{35}$	1	Accept equivalent fractions.	T
8	1.838	1		T
9	78	1		T
10	11,087	1		T
11	49	1		E
12	87.333 (recurring)	2	Award **2 marks** for the correct answer of **87.33**. If the answer is incorrect, award **1 mark** for a formal method of division with no more than **one** arithmetical error.	G
13	0.7	1		E
14	144	1		E
15	1,701	1		E
16	$\frac{9}{4}$ or $2\frac{1}{4}$	1	Accept equivalent mixed numbers, fractions or an **exact** decimal equivalent, e.g. 2.25 (accept any unambiguous indication of the recurring digit).	E
17	$\frac{1}{27}$	1	Accept equivalent fractions.	E
18	$\frac{5}{48}$	1	Accept equivalent fractions.	E
19	498,168	2	Award **2 marks** for the correct answer of 498,168. If the answer is incorrect, award **1 mark** for a formal method of long multiplication with no more than **one** arithmetical error.	G
20	174	1		E
21	8	1		E
22	51	1		E
23	444.4	1		E
24	2,020	1		E
25	121	1		E
26	0.458	1		E
27	$10\frac{1}{12}$ or $\frac{121}{12}$	1	Accept equivalent mixed numbers, fractions or decimal equivalent, e.g. 10.0833 (accept any unambiguous indication of the recurring digit).	G
28	$\frac{3}{14}$	1	Accept equivalent fractions.	E

Year 6 Summer Half Term 2: Arithmetic Mark Scheme

29	350	1		E
30	4,297	1	Accept 4297 written without commas.	E
31	468.93	1		E
32	100.9	1		E
33	$\frac{10}{91}$	1	Accept equivalent fractions.	E
34	773.5	1		G
35	748,020	2	Award **2 marks** for the correct answer of 748,020. If the answer is incorrect, award **1 mark** for a formal method of long multiplication with no more than **one** arithmetical error	G
36	39.75	2	Award **2 marks** for the correct answer of 39.75. If the answer is incorrect, award **1 mark** for a formal method of division with no more than **one** arithmetical error.	G

Threshold scores

Working towards the expected standard: 23 or fewer
Working at the expected standard: 24–31
Working at greater depth: 32–40

Balance of difficulty of questions in the paper

10 marks at working towards (T)
20 marks at the expected standard (E)
10 marks at working at greater depth (G)

Year 6 Summer Half Term 2: Reasoning Mark Scheme

Question	Requirement	Mark	Additional guidance	Level of demand
1	Point marked 8.6 cm from point A.	1	Accept any clear indication of the point marked if it is at the correct point.	T
2	3,750 m	2	Award **2 marks** for the correct answer of 3,750 m. If incorrect, award **1 mark** for evidence of a correct method.	T
3	261 tubs	2	Award **2 marks** for the correct answer of 261 tubs. If incorrect, award **1 mark** for evidence of a correct method.	T
4a 4b	3 minutes 52 seconds 5 minutes 7 seconds	1 1		T
5	Only three correct boxes ticked: 2, 4, 8	2	Award **2 marks** for only three correct boxes ticked. Award **1 mark** for only two correct boxes ticked and no incorrect boxes ticked **or** three correct boxes ticked and one incorrect box ticked.	T
6	All four completed correctly. 12 3 6 5	2	Award **2 marks** for all four completed correctly. Award **1 mark** for three correctly completed. Also accept 12,000,000 300,000 6,000 500 written correctly.	E
7	5,806 cars	3	Award **2 marks** for the correct answer of 5,806 cars. Award **2 marks** for evidence of three correct numbers added together 1898 + 2115 + 1793 Award **1 mark** for evidence of an appropriate method which contains more than **one** arithmetical error.	E
8	All four boxes correct. < > < =	2	Award **2 marks** for all four boxes correct. Award **1 mark** if one incorrect but three boxes correct.	E
9	$\dfrac{1}{12}$	1	Award **1 mark** for identifying that he eats $\dfrac{1}{12}$ of each pizza, so he eats $\dfrac{1}{12}$ of the available pizza (2 pizzas) altogether.	E
10	£9.36	2	Award **2 marks** for the correct answer of £9.36. If incorrect, award **1 mark** for evidence of a correct method.	G
11a 11b	Area = base × height ($A = b \times h$) 37.5 cm^2	1 1		E

Year 6 Summer Half Term 2: Reasoning Mark Scheme

12	6,744 cars	3	Award **3 marks** for the correct answer of 6,744 cars. If the answer is incorrect, award **2 marks** for sight of 18,780 for the first step completed correctly. **or** evidence of an appropriate method which contains no more than **one** arithmetical error. Award **1 mark** for evidence of an appropriate method which contains more than **one** arithmetical error.	G
13	No. Explanation should identify that to find volume it should be $l \times w \times h$.	1		E
14	15.2 m	3	Award **3 marks** for correct answer of 15.2 m. If incorrect, award **2 marks** for correct identification of both amounts 12.8 m and 4 m. Award **1 mark** for evidence of an appropriate method which contains more than **one** arithmetical error.	G
15	$\dfrac{1}{5}$	1	Also accept 0.2.	E
16	$(6 \times 8 = 48) + 5 = 53$. Explanation should show that the multiplication should be done before the addition.	1		E
17	£123.46.	3	Award **3 marks** for the correct answer of £123.46. If incorrect, award **2 marks** for the correct identification of 1728.44 divided by 14 but incorrect answer. Award **1 mark** for evidence of correct addition but errors with division.	G
18	200 cm^3	2	Award **2 marks** for the correct answer of 200 cm^3. If incorrect, award **1 mark** for evidence of a correct method.	E

Threshold scores
Working towards the expected standard: 20 or fewer
Working at the expected standard: 21–27
Working at greater depth: 28–35

Balance of difficulty of questions in the paper
9 marks at working towards (T)
15 marks at the expected standard (E)
11 marks at working at greater depth (G)

Content domain references

Autumn 1: Arithmetic

Question	Content domain ref.
1	4C6b
2	3C7
3	3C1
4	3F4
5	4C2
6	4C7
7	3N2b
8	5F10
9	5C5d
10	5C6a
11	6C9
12	6C6
13	5C6b
14	6C7c
15	4C6a
16	5C7b
17	5F4
18	5C2
19	5C7a
20	6C9
21	4C6b
22	6C6
23	6C7c
24	6C9
25	6C9, 5C5d
26	6C7c
27	6C7a
28	6C9, 5C5d
29	6C7a
30	6C7b
31	6N3
32	6N3

Autumn 1: Reasoning

Question	Content domain ref.
1	3N2b
2	3C2, 3C3
3	4C4
4	4C6a
5	6C5
6	5C1
7	5N2
8	5N1
9	6N5

10	5N3b
11	6C8
12	6N4
13	6C8
14	6C5
15	6N2
16	6C8
17	6C8
18	6C6
19	6N6

Autumn 2: Arithmetic

Question	Content domain ref.
1	4N2b
2	4F8, 4C2
3	5C2
4	5C7b
5	5F8
6	5C6b
7	5F8
8	4F4
9	6N6
10	6N2
11	6C9
12	5F5
13	6N6
14	4C7
15	5F5
16	6F5a
17	6F5b
18	6C9, 5C5d
19	5F10
20	6C9
21	6F4
22	6C9, 5C5d
23	5F4
24	6C9
25	65Fb
26	65Fb
27	6F4
28	6F4
29	6c7b/c
30	6c7a
31	6c7b/c
32	6N3

Autumn 2: Reasoning

Question	Content domain ref.
1	4F2
2	4C8
3	5C8a, 5C7a
4	5N3a
5	5F10
6	5F12
7	6C8
8	6F4
9	6F2
10	6C3
11	6C5
12	6F11/6F3
13	6P2
14	6F9a/5C6b
15	6C8
16	6C6
17	5M7b/5C7a
18	6P3

Content domain references

Spring 1: Arithmetic	
Question	Content domain ref.
1	3F4
2	3N2b
3	4C7
4	4N2b
5	4F4
6	5F4
7	5F5
8	5C6a
9	5F8
10	5F4
11	5F10
12	6F9a
13	6R2
14	6C9
15	6F5b
16	6F4
17	6C9
18	6F9b
19	6F5b
20	6F9a
21	6F5a
22	6F9b
23	6C9
24	6F4
25	6F5a
26	6R2
27	6F9a
28	6F4
29	6F9b
30	6R2
31	6C7b/c
32	6C7a
33	6C7b/c
34	6C7a
35	6N3
36	6N3

Spring 1: Reasoning	
Question	Content domain ref.
1	4F10b
2	4P2
3	5C5a/b/c
4	5F10
5	5F8
6a 6b	6N5
7	6N2
8	6R2
9	6A5
10	6F3, 6F2
11a 11b	6A1
12a 12b	6A4
13	5F12
14	6F9a, 5C6b
15a 15b	6A2
16	6F6
17	6F11
18	6A2
19	6R1

Spring 2: Arithmetic	
Question	Content domain ref.
1	3N2b
2	4C2
3	4C6b
4	4C7
5	5C5d
6	5F5
7	5C5d
8	5F8
9	5C2
10	5F4
11	5F5
12	6C9
13	6R2
14	6F9b
15	6F5a
16	6F9a
17	6R2
18	6F9a
19	6F4
20	6R2
21	6F5b

22	6C9
23	6F5b
24	6F4
25	6F9b
26	6R2
27	6F5b
28	6C9, 5C5d
29	6R2
30	6C7a
31	6C7b/c
32	6C7a
33	6C7b/c
34	6N3
35	6N3
36	6N3

Spring 2: Reasoning	
Question	Content domain ref.
1	4M4c
2	4M4b
3	5M8
4	5F10
5	5M9b/6R3
6	5M9a
7	5M5, 5C8a
8	6R1
9	6F10
10	6R2
11a 11b	6M5
12	6F9
13	6R1
14	6M8a
15a 15b	6M7a
16	6R4
17	6M7b
18	6R3
19	5M7b/5C7a

Content domain references

Summer 1: Arithmetic

Question	Content domain ref.
1	4C6b
2	4C6a
3	4C2
4	4F8, 4C2
5	5C6b
6	5C5d
7	5C2
8	5F10
9	5F5
10	5C6b
11	5F8, 5F2
12	6F9a
13	6C9
14	6R2
15	6F4
16	6F9b
17	6F5b
18	6C7b/c
19	6F5a
20	6R2
21	6F4
22	6F5a
23	6F5b
24	6C7a
25	6C9
26	6F9b
27	6F9a
28	6F5a
29	6R2
30	6F5b
31	6F4
32	6C7a
33	6C7b/c
34	6N3
35	6N3
36	6N3

Summer 1: Reasoning

Question	Content domain ref.
1a 1b	4S1
2	4G2c
3	5F10
4	5C2
5	5S1
6	5G4c
7	6S3, 6C8
8	6M6
9	6G3a
10	6G4a, 4G2a
11	6S1
12	6G2a
13	6S3
14a 14b	6G3b
15	6G2b
16a 16b	6G4
17	6R3
18	6G5
19	6F4/6A3
20	6F4

Summer 2: Arithmetic

Question	Content domain ref.
1	4F4
2	4C7
3	5F10
4	5C5d
5	5C2
6	5C6a
7	5F4
8	5F8
9	5F5
10	5C2
11	6C9
12	6C7b/c
13	6F9a
14	6R2
15	6F9b
16	6F4
17	6F5b
18	6F5a
19	6C7a
20	6C9, 5C5d
21	6F4

22	6C9
23	6F9b
24	6R2
25	6C9
26	6F9a
27	6F4
28	6F5a
29	6R2
30	6C9
31	6F9b
32	6F9a
33	6F5b
34	6R2
35	6C7a
36	6C7b/c

Summer 2: Reasoning

Question	Content domain ref.
1	3M2a
2	4F10a
3	5F5
4a 4b	5M4
5	5C5a
6	6N3
7	6C4
8	6C6
9	6F5a
10	6F9c
11a 11b	6M7b/c
12	6C7a
13	6M8b
14	6M9
15	6F5b
16	6C9
17	6C8/6C7b/c
18	6M8a

Name _____   Class _____

Year 6/P7 Maths Progress Tests for White Rose Record Sheet

Tests	Mark	Total marks	Key skills to target
Autumn 1: Arithmetic			
Autumn 1: Reasoning			
Autumn 2: Arithmetic			
Autumn 2: Reasoning			
Spring 1: Arithmetic			
Spring 1: Reasoning			
Spring 2: Arithmetic			
Spring 2: Reasoning			
Summer 1: Arithmetic			
Summer 1: Reasoning			
Summer 2: Arithmetic			
Summer 2: Reasoning			